HOW
to Feel
MANLY
in a
MINIVAN

THE DESPERATE DAD'S
SURVIVAL GUIDE

St. Martin's Griffin ❧ New York

HOW
to Feel
MANLY
in a
MINIVAN

Craig Boreth

*Illustrations by
Jay Mazhar*

www.stmartins.com

Title page illustration copyright © 2007 by Jay Mazhar.

Book design by Jennifer Ann Daddio

Library of Congress Cataloging-in-Publication Data

Boreth, Craig.
    How to feel manly in a minivan / Craig Boreth.—
1st St. Martin's Griffin ed.
        p. cm.
    ISBN-13: 978-0-312-36312-3
    ISBN-10: 0-312-36312-5
    1. Fatherhood. 2. Fathers—Psychology.
3. Husbands—Psychology. 4. Parenting. 5. Pregnancy. 6. Father and infant. I. Title.

HQ756.B664 2007
306.874'2—dc22

                                                  2007004299

First Edition: May 2007

1   3   5   7   9   0   2   4   6   8

For My Dad,

WHO OBVIOUSLY DID A DAMN FINE JOB,

and For My Son,

WHO I HOPE SOMEDAY CAN SAY THE SAME.

CONTENTS

CONTENTS

A BOOK INSTEAD
OF BOOZE

As a matter of principle, I don't buy gifts for babies. I refuse to give a present to someone who doesn't yet have reliable sphincter control but already has a larger wardrobe than I do. Even before they're born, babies begin to accumulate staggering quantities of stuff, and it keeps coming pretty much unabated throughout their first year. The deluge seems inexorably drawn to the baby, like mall cops to Winona Ryder. On that note, when Ms. Ryder found out how much free swag babies get just by being born, she immediately ran out and tried to be born again. Unfortunately, the church elders couldn't forgive her past transgressions, most notably that performance in *Mr. Deeds*.

As I see it, babies have got a pretty sweet gig just sitting around being waited on hand and foot while Mom and Dad go nuts. Therefore, when I need to get a gift, I'd much rather get one for the folks who've really earned it: the parents. And when shopping for new parents, there's only one logical choice of gift: the gift that keeps on giving. The gift that says, "I feel your pain, and I've got the cure." That's right: booze.

Whether it's a nice bottle of wine for those all-too-rare quiet dinners together, a single-malt Scotch for sipping in a comfy chair with a good book, or an immense jug of cheap vodka for swilling like a Russian longshoreman, nothing expresses my sympathy for the new parents' predicament better than a bottle of booze. Of course, since I've become a parent myself and have graduated from sympathizing to empathizing, I've changed my attitude slightly. These days I give what I believe to be a much better gift: even more booze.

As much as I'd like to send each and every new parent out there a desperately needed bottle of benumbing spirits, it simply isn't practical. Believe me, I tried, but the promo department at St. Martin's balked at the suggestion. Of course, that didn't keep them from accepting delivery on free samples from Seagram's, Grey Goose, Stoli, Bacardi, Olde English 800, Maker's Mark, Patrón, those wacky alchemists at Jägermeister, and the lesser-known German brand Aufdiebrettermitschwungtrunk (which roughly translates as "drink that swiftly lets you greet the floor"). So instead of alcohol, I figured a book would be the next best thing.

I soon found out that writing a book for parents is a lot like buying a gift for a baby. Just as it's difficult to find a gift that the baby doesn't already have, it's hard to think of information that isn't already available from any number of other sources. There are so many books out there specifically intended to teach parents how to care for their children, I couldn't possibly add anything of value to that pile. Of the books that focus on the parents' well-being, the vast majority of them are written for mothers. Since my experience as a mother is figurative at best, I figured the best I could do was to share everything I've learned about the art of fatherly self-preservation.

So I offer to my fellow fathers this little book of friendly advice, suggestions, and best wishes for smooth travels. I hope it's an adequate substitute for that bottle of booze, taking the edge off the whole process, giving you a boost of courage, and leaving you feeling just a bit goofy. I apologize in advance if it leaves you with a killer headache afterward.

WHO THE BOOK IS FOR

I've tried to make this book at least somewhat helpful to as many guys facing fatherhood as possible. While no two guys deal with becoming a dad in quite the same way, there are certain situations that most of us will find ourselves in, and I hope this book will get you through them a bit more easily. I'm working under the assumption that you're in a reasonably stable and committed relationship. Throughout the book I refer to your significant other as your wife, but frankly it really doesn't matter if you're married or not, or even if your wife is a woman.

Of course, there are many men who come to fatherhood under more difficult circumstances, men whose unfathomable needs cannot possibly be addressed by any single book. For example, I can't imagine how someone deals with becoming a parent by accident. The best I can do is recommend extensive therapy and heavy sedation. I also can't comprehend how any sentient adult could want to have a baby to try and save a failing relationship. Those guys are more delusional than an optimistic Cubs fan. Finally, to any single fathers out there, you have my deepest admiration. How you survive at all is right up there with the Big Bang and Donald Trump's hair on my list of inexplicable phenomena.

Difficulty/Reward Ratings

If you're anything like me, you probably approach many of life's tasks with the goal of getting them done with the minimum exertion possible. Some would call that lazy. I prefer to think of it as shrewdly efficient. Either way, fatherhood is no different. To help you achieve this state of maximum efficiency, I've included Difficulty and Reward ratings for each tutorial in the book. That way, you can determine which tasks will return the best reward (in terms of your paternal pride, free time, and/or sanity) based on the amount of effort expended.

The rating system is very simple. The difficulty of a task is indicated by one to four baby bottles, and your reward is indicated by one to four beer bottles. Obviously, those entries with more beer bottles than milk bottles are the most rewarding. As for those difficult tasks that offer little reward, they're the chores you just have to do, and I hope knowing that beforehand can make them a bit more bearable.

The Therapy Jar

I've tried to be completely honest and open with you on the subject of father-hood. Unfortunately, in some cases having done so will no doubt cause my own son great embarrassment someday. In anticipation of the mental anguish he'll no doubt suffer, and to relieve my guilt at the torment I'll cause him, I've created a "Therapy Jar," into which I make donations from time to time. So, next to certain passages in the book you'll see the therapy jar, increasingly full of the money it will take to deal with the various neuroses those passages are likely to instill. And it's not just for me. Someday, your kid might read this book and infer what a screwup you were when he was born. And when that day comes you'll be glad you set aside a therapy jar to cover the costs.

HOW
to Feel
MANLY
in a
MINIVAN

Greetings from your future! I'm speaking to you now from that curious, often stupefying state commonly known as fatherhood. While I can hardly remember what my everyday life was like before the baby—for example, I've no idea how I occupied myself during the many hours every day that are now taken up with baby-related activities—I can clearly recall that I found the prospect of fatherhood intimidating as hell.

But sitting here now, having been through it all and feeling reasonably comfortable and confident as a father, I'm reminded of a quote from the movie *The Man Who Wasn't There*:

While you're in the maze, you go through it willy-nilly, turn-ing where you think you have to turn, banging into the dead ends, one thing after another. But you get some distance on it, and all those twists and turns . . . why, they're the shape of your life.

As you embark upon your great adventure toward fatherhood, marked most notably by what is in all likelihood your very first experience with meaningful sex (see "How to Have Sex for Pro-creation"), remember that while you may just be a rat in a maze with no clue where you are, sooner or later, one way or another, you'll reach the cheese. Happy trails.

HOW TO ABANDON YOUR ENTIRE EXISTENCE

Everything changes.

—PROVERB OF FATHERHOOD (ORIGIN TWENTIETH CENTURY AMERICAN: DISGRUNTLED DADS)

Most guys aren't big on change. Given the choice, they'd probably prefer a full body wax to changing even one insignificant part of their lives. The prospect of *everything* changing sends many guys off to a quiet place and, ironically, the fetal position. Fatherhood, of course, represents just such a comprehensive transformation.

Abandon hope all ye who enter here

MATERNITY

They say that ignorance is bliss, but for a reasonably content guy facing the unknown perils of fatherhood, ignorance is terrifying. He imagines a future awash in dirty diapers, sleepless nights, and soul-crushing responsibilities, all leading eventually to the sweet release of senility. It's a pretty bleak picture indeed, and one that most guys can't imagine themselves surviving with any sense of dignity. But face it, your life is always changing, and you've always adjusted. Remember when you first left for college? That was a pretty significant shift in your life, and at the time I'll bet you felt really out of sorts (at least I hope you did, and you weren't one of those cool kids who adjusted instantly and started bedding coeds before Parents' Weekend. Not that I'm jealous.). But you adjusted, and after a while you couldn't imagine going back to your old life.

Of course, having a kid isn't exactly like heading off to college, except for the all-nighters, the vomiting, and the general bewilderment. Becoming a father is probably the most dramatic, instantaneous change in a man's life since he himself was born. It's a thoroughly transformative experience, like his wedding day, his first sexual experience, and his first trip to a Panamanian brothel all rolled into one. And every time someone tells you that "everything changes," you assume that the statement is filled with regret, and that all fathers wish they could go back to the days before it all changed. It's the belief that you will soon find yourself hopelessly nostalgic for what once was, regardless of how delusional that desire may be, that prompts so many men to fear the prospect of everything changing.

One suggestion I have for guys who tremble at the prospect of fatherhood is to ask yourself if you would really go back to a previous time in your life. Let me qualify that: Would you go back and live it the same way again, *without* knowing what you know now, and therefore *not* getting laid a lot more often than you did the first time? I think most guys are happy to keep moving forward, and becoming a father is just the latest in a long line of constant life changes. You'll get used to fatherhood just like you got used to everything else. Don't believe me? Here's an example that shows just how adaptable we humans can be.

In 1896, Berkeley psychologist George Stratton published the findings from a study in which he wore mirror glasses that inverted his view of the world. For three weeks, his perception of the world was literally turned upside-down. At first he'd get nauseous whenever he moved his head, let alone when he tried (and failed) to walk. But after about a week, his eyes and brain adjusted so that he saw the world as "normal" again, and was able to function as he had without the glasses.

That's pretty much what happens when you become a father. Your world is turned upside-down, you're queasy for a while, and just about every aspect of your life is different than it was before the baby. But quickly enough, you'll adjust and everything will seem normal once again. I'm not saying your life won't be crazy, frustrating, and exhausting, but it's still your life, and trust me, you'll get used to it.

And not only will you get used to it, but before long you may actually grow to enjoy it, and you won't be willing to trade your life as a father for anything. I hope this book will help you get to that point just a little bit more quickly, because the sooner you get there, the easier the whole fatherhood thing becomes. And as we'll see, you can't fake it (nor should you); you really have to feel it. But for now, you've got some mental gymnastics to do if you're going to be able to think of yourself as a father without shrieking like a schoolgirl. So let's get started.

HOW TO REINFORCE THE DELUSION THAT YOU'RE READY

Difficulty   *Reward*

Am I not a man? And is not a man stupid? I'm a man.
So I married. Wife, children, house, everything.
The full catastrophe.

—ZORBA (ANTHONY QUINN), *ZORBA THE GREEK*

Before you and your wife even thought of having a baby, you probably looked at your friends with kids and thought about what their lives had become. In your mind, you saw them reduced to little more than groveling attendants pandering to the whims of those ungrateful little homunculi. Their lives seemed to consist of nothing more than dirty diapers, strained carrots, and slobbery plastic toys. Put yourself in their shoes and you won't be able to get your head in the oven fast enough.

Let's just take a deep breath, turn off the gas, grab a beer, and assess the situation. You can't possibly be mature enough to be a father, right? You've got so much more living to do before settling down, right? Your wife may leave voice mail messages with nothing except her saying "tick-tock-tick-tock" over and over again, but you're just not ready.

The fact is that nobody, male or female, is ever truly ready to have kids. And those who believe they're ready usually end up on the local news a few years down the road talking forthrightly about how little Bobby was such a sweet child, and how that pentagram burned into the neighbor's yard just couldn't be his handiwork. Our only job here is to get you as ready as you can be, since eventually you're going to wake up one day and find that it's too late, and you're already a father.

First, let's take a moment to figure out exactly *why* guys have such a tough time relating to babies. Most modern guys feel that they don't have much in common with babies. Men do not openly express emotions, whereas babies do nothing but that. For most men, crying has been completely expunged from their emotional vernacular. And with the exception of recent fraternity initiates and Howard Stern interns, most men haven't defiled a diaper in a long, long time. You can't possibly expect men to understand a creature that would refuse to eat or sleep whenever it has the chance. I mean, that's just crazy. Finally, most men feel that the closer they get to a baby, the more they lose control and risk embarrassment or irreversible feminization.

In fact, a Canadian study actually found that men's testosterone levels dropped by as much as one-third after their babies were born, and the larger the decrease, the more protective the father. (On a barely related note, other Canadian researchers found that herring communicate by farting. If that doesn't prove we're all descended from a common ancestor, nothing does.) Let's face it: babies exist in a primarily feminine domain, and for good reason. The human male's natural state is no place for small children. (In my research for this book, though, I did discover many previously overlooked ways in which men can relate to babies. See "The Mothering Male.")

Naturally some men will try to overcome their hesitancy about babies by spending time with a few. Big mistake. Playing dad with somebody else's kid is the single worst thing you can do when trying to convince yourself that you're ready to be a dad yourself. Maybe you'll babysit for a few hours or, worse yet, agree to take the kid for an entire day. Let me save you the trouble of actually embarking on this endeavor and tell you how it's going to turn out. You're going to end up a bitter, angry, thoroughly exhausted and dispirited shell of your former self. And you'll be even more convinced that you're not ready. Why is that? Simply put, because it's not your kid.

Here's proof that dealing with your own baby versus someone else's makes all the difference: before I became a father, I was unsure about whether I'd be a good father, and I was thoroughly unenthusiastic about babies in general. I didn't mind spending time with babies, but given the choice I would rather they kept their distance. Now, by comparison, I consider myself a very competent and enthusiastic father, I'm completely comfortable taking care of my son, and I love spending time with him. I logically assumed that I had developed some new appreciation for babies in general. Nope. I still feel exactly the same way about other babies as I did before.

What this all means is that accepting fatherhood is really just a leap of faith, like raising blind in poker or ordering chicken in Chinatown. You just need to believe that it will all work out, and try to embrace the whole epic journey. Remember all those years ago when you made that bold move and lost your virginity? It's a little bit like that, except in this case you don't have the opportunity to practice extensively on your own ahead of time.

One way to make that leap a bit easier is to realize that babies are actually more similar to men than they are to women. Sure, babies are as incomprehensible as women, you can never quite tell exactly what they want, and they'll ruin your golf game, but they also burp and fart all the time and giggle at even the most ridiculous sight gags. You've managed to figure out women sufficiently to get within boinking range of at least one of them. How hard can it be to figure out a baby? In actuality, convincing a woman to bear your progeny is like cracking the Nazis' Enigma codes compared to understanding your baby.

Total Commitment

At some point along the way to fatherhood you'll feel like there's no turning back and you've made a huge mistake. When that happens, think back on the other times when you've felt this way about major life commitments, like when you got married, when you bought a house, or when you started watching the latest season of *24*. In those cases, you could've turned back if you really wanted to, and that can actually make it more stressful. With fatherhood, you *really* can't turn back. Like General Ripper said in *Dr. Strangelove*: you've got no choice except "total commitment." And, sometimes, having no choice at all can make commitment pretty easy.

The next step is to figure out how to make the transition to fatherhood as smooth and easy as possible. First, it might be helpful to think about fatherhood as being biologically inevitable. During the pregnancy, you'll be amazed as you learn about all of the innumerable developmental processes that take place. It's hard to believe that everything that must happen actually does, and the end result is a little mini-human with two eyes, ten fingers, and little hobbit feet. And yet, somehow, in most cases it all happens just right. It's enough to almost make an old agnostic believe in some higher power. Almost.

Your development as a father will progress just as inexorably. The pregnancy gives you nine months to start getting ready, safely protected from the actual realities of parenthood. After the baby is born, your fatherhood skills will develop just as quickly as the baby does.

I remember a friend once telling a worried new parent that all healthy kids learn to walk and talk eventually. After all, you don't see many adults who never picked up those skills. Although you could make a case for Paris Hilton, who speaks in an infantile babble and spends way too much time on her back. (Thank you, ladies and gentlemen. I'll be here all week.) The point I was trying to make before I was so easily distracted is that becoming a father is as inevitable for you as learning to walk and talk are for your baby. Eventually, everybody figures it out.

I think one way new fathers get themselves into trouble is to think about their own fathers. They think, *As far back as I can remember, my dad always seemed to know what he was doing, and yet I feel totally unprepared.* The problem with this line of reasoning is that you can only remember your dad about as far back as when you were four or five. So as a new father, you've actually got a couple of years before you really need to get your act together. And you've got about ten years before the kid finds some photos from college and asks you about those funny little cigarettes you smoked back then. And from that point it's a couple more years before he finds out just how big a screwup you were when you were his age, and wonders if he'll ever be ready to be a dad himself. And so the miraculous cycle repeats itself down through the generations.

Finally, you need to trust your instincts, although you may rightfully doubt that human males actually harbor any. In addition to the portrayal on every sitcom since the dawn of television, there's actually evidence in the slightly more relevant field of evolutionary biology to suggest that human males are less than perfectly suited to parenthood. When we look at mammals in general, we see that only about 5 percent exhibit any degree of paternal care for newborns, and those mammals that do exhibit paternal nurturing tend to be rather less than awesome creatures, like prairie voles or hippies. In other classes of animals, where the female isn't bound to nursing by virtue of her mammary glands, there are more examples of paternal care. These include marine worms, water bugs, sea horses, and most birds, including penguins.

So it seems logical to conclude that paternal nurturing is usually relegated to animals that aren't exactly what you'd call top-of-the-food-chain types. You won't see car companies scrambling to name new models after these animals. You're never going to see a Buick Prairie Vole or the Chevy Water Bug. (Although I may be giving GM too much credit. Anyone remember the Pontiac Parisienne?)

Modern man may try to use this example to absolve himself of any parenting responsibility. After all, aren't women evolutionarily better suited to parenthood? I mean, isn't that why every time you read about really cool animals like lions, hippos, and badgers ripping an unsuspecting hiker to ribbons for crossing between them and their young, it's usually the females doing the disemboweling? Nice try, guys, but sometimes even the best logic falls flat when confronted by reality.

And the reality is that suburban living, technology, and salty snack foods have softened up the modern man. We've been domesticated, and that means we have no excuse for being poor parents. On the positive side, that means we are in fact perfectly capable of being good parents. And yes, that also means that sitcoms may not be an accurate reflection of reality. I realize that may come as a shock, but you're better off knowing the truth.

All that being said, let's not get cocky. Becoming a father is one of the more difficult endeavors you'll embark upon in your life. Don't expect that when the baby arrives you'll jump right in and be perfectly comfortable in your new role. You will, though, be good enough at it to keep you and your baby relatively sane, and keep you off of your local Child Services agent's "to do" list. And just as your child will develop and mature at an astonishingly fast rate in the early months of his life, so, too, will you develop as a father. Of course, it is a never-ending process, and there's always more growing to do. For example, to this day, when someone calls me Daddy, I look around for my own father. They can't possibly be talking about me, can they? I'm still just not ready.

The Mothering Male

Before your baby is even born, you'll no doubt tire of all the chatter about how women are more naturally suited to parenthood than men (you may even find some such flapdoodle in this very book). Sure, women are capable of growing an entire human being inside their bodies; they can nourish that human once he's born with manna brought forth from their breasts; and they possess a seemingly limitless wellspring of glorious and flawless maternal love. But what about us guys? You hardly ever hear any discussion of the myriad ways in which men are innately well suited to parenthood. That is, until now.

Fathers need to recognize that they see the world in much the same way their baby does, and take advantage of that fact. For example, babies can produce some of the vilest odors known to man. And yet they just sit there within that typhoon of stank, breaking occasionally into a devilish giggle. Now you tell me, who does that remind you of? This is just one example within the broad category of phenomena—namely, potty humor—about which men and babies share an almost identical interpretation. Of course, women may speak derisively of this type of humor, but I'm pretty sure they're just jealous of our unspoken connection with the baby.

Besides the fact that babies almost always speak their daddy's name first (see "How to Make Sure the Baby Says 'Daddy' First," to ensure that he does), there's an earlier form of communication that hints at the innate bond between father and child. One of the first gestures that a baby will intentionally mimic is the "raspberry" (that's right, we're still in the realm of ass). There must be a reason why this gesture, still considered humorous by so many adult males, is among the earliest forms of communication between parent and child (I have absolutely no idea what that reason is, but I'm sure there is one).

Finally, recent studies have shown that a baby's developing immune system benefits from early exposure to allergens, bacteria, and other everyday detritus. The theory is that a baby's immune system doesn't yet know which invaders need to be taken seriously. As it gets exposed early on to mostly harmless things like dust, dirt, and Doritos crumbs, it figures out pretty quickly that these things aren't too bad and develops the proper resistance to them. If babies are not exposed to these things early enough, their immune systems can mature without the proper resistance, and they become more likely to develop allergies and other negative reactions.

Basically what this all means is not only that the five-second rule has been totally vindicated (and should probably be changed to the five-minute rule), it also shows that men are naturally more attuned to their baby's needs in this case. After all, who is more likely to look out for the best interest of the child: a mother who washes her hands before touching the baby and keeps the house spotless, or a father who believes that the best way to improve interspecies relations is to let the baby and the dog share their chew toys? My vote, and the research backs me up on this, goes to Dad.

HOW TO HAVE SEX FOR PROCREATION PART 1: PREPARATION

Difficulty   *Reward*

Nothing signals the onset of true adulthood like having meaningful sex. Unfortunately, if your wife is to become impregnated, with you as the father, you're going to have to give it a shot. For most guys, "meaningful sex" is as baffling an oxymoron as "veggie burger" or "sincere apology." For much of our lives, sex was just the end by which all sneaky, dishonest, and borderline felonious means were justified. There were no other goals besides the sex itself, except possibly to *not* get her pregnant. Suddenly your primary objective is exactly that which you've worked so hard to avoid. Your whole coital reality has been turned upside-down, and you find yourself in virgin territory once again (so to speak). This time, there couldn't be bigger consequences to the sex, and avoiding pregnancy is the last thing on your mind (I hope). It's enough to trigger a nasty case of hysterical impotence (although I, of course, have no direct experience with such afflictions).

Before we get into the plan of attack for this particular mission, let's take a moment to make sure that all the manly ordnance is in proper working order. While some of you may think that frequent, mandatory sex is a dream come true, let me assure you that the gilding falls off that particular lily pretty quickly. And the longer you go without success, the more stressful it becomes, until eventually you may wilt under the pressure (quite literally). So let's make sure you're in peak physical condition for the task at hand.

Basic Training

WATCH YOUR WEIGHT

Despite all the perks, making a baby is tough work. You want to be as fit as possible. To make matters worse, large deposits of fat can cause the body to transform male hormones into estrogen, which will slow the production of sperm. On a related note, you don't want to cut too much fat out of your diet (hello, Atkins!), which can result in lower testosterone levels. On another related note, if you're exercising to lose weight, try not to overdo it. Some studies have shown that excessive exercise can lower sperm count and testosterone levels. This may be caused by the fact that strenuous workouts can cause overheating, which is also why you shouldn't use a sauna or spa for at least a few months before you start trying.

WEAR WHAT YOU WANT

There's been much debate about the relative impact of boxers versus briefs on male fertility. Common sense suggests that you don't want too much restriction down there, but the research is inconclusive, so either one is fine. What is certain is that it's much more difficult to get the wife turned on in tighty-whities (for future reference).

MULTIVITAMINS

If you're not taking a multivitamin, such as One-A-Day for Men, you should be, regardless of whether or not you're trying to knock up the wife. With pregnancy on the agenda, you definitely should be supplementing. Vitamin C keeps your sperm mobile, zinc can increase semen volume, and vitamins A, E, and beta-carotene help fight the chemicals that can damage sperm.

THE OBVIOUS STUFF

Cut back on the booze and stop smoking. While drinking may have played an essential role in previous sexual forays, it's definitely detrimental during meaningful sex. As we'll see later, you should cut back on your drinking during her pregnancy anyway (see "How to Help Her Get off the Sauce"), so you might as well start now. And, of course, you should definitely stop smoking, as it's almost as bad for your sperm as it is for your lungs.

SLIP 'N' SLIDE

Finally, avoid using lubricant, which can kill sperm. Instead, use Johnson's Baby Oil. If that doesn't kill your mood, you should have no trouble sowing your seeds.

Now that you've made it through basic training, it's time for deployment.

HOW TO HAVE SEX FOR PROCREATION PART 2: DOING THE DEED

Difficulty (the sex part)

(the fertilization part)

Reward

Before I even begin, this chapter calls for a major donation to the Therapy Jar.

I'm not going to get into the gory details of the act itself; that's between you, your wife, and guy at the Photomat. One thing that I will suggest is that you check out a great book, *Taking Charge of Your Fertility* by Toni Weschler. Even if you don't anticipate any problems conceiving, this book will give you a great feeling of control over the whole process. Plus, you'll begin to get some sense of the amazing baby-making machine that is your wife. And, trust me on this, the more familiar you become with how your wife works (physically, that is; her mind will always be impenetrable), the better off you'll be when moving forward.

As the "big bang" approaches, many men feel conflicted. On the one hand, they want to, as the folks at NASA would put it, "impart sufficient thrust to achieve escape velocity," but doing so usually requires a particularly enthusiastic, bestial commitment to the task at hand. Given the circumstances, it's difficult to channel your inner porn star, especially with cute, cuddly images of your future progeny floating through your head. It's as if he's already in the room with you, and that's really disturbing. (Actually, that idea could make for a really perverse fetish flick: Your child comes back from the future and walks in on you and your wife conceiving him. You could call it *The Sperminator*. Do thoughts like that make me a really bad person? Just in case, I'll drop $20 in the Therapy Jar.)

 Basically, the only advice I can give to help you succeed in this task is to dip into your supply of what little machismo and insensitivity you've got left after just a few years of marriage, and get right down to it. This is definitely one time when men's complete disconnect from our own emotions comes in handy. I'd refrain from any dirty talk, though. After all, that's the mother of your child you're talking to. And after it's over, you should probably try and stay awake at least until she finishes sobbing.

Welcome to our world, my friend, for today you are a man.

Pregger Pops

Let me clear up a common misconception that you may hold regarding having sex while your wife is pregnant (that is, having sex *with* your wife while she's pregnant). I'm not sure whether it's due to gross overestimation of one's endowment or gross ignorance of the female anatomy (or some combination of the two), but many men believe that they'll somehow injure the baby while having sex while their wife is pregnant. Rest assured that in almost all cases sex during pregnancy is perfectly safe, and unless you get that anatomically impossible image out of your head right away, you won't be enjoying sex for a long, long time.

So, not only can you have sex during pregnancy, but you may actually find that pregnancy offers certain advantages. First and foremost, the hormones raging through your wife's body can boost her sex drive. More importantly, those hormones may also allow her to enjoy sex more (or, in some cases, enjoy it at all). As you can see, rather than suffering through a 9-month nooky drought while your wife is pregnant, you may end up enjoying an unprecedented run of near-constant, wife-satisfying coitus.

HOW YOUR BABY IS LIKE A PET AND A COLLEGE ROOMMATE

Much of men's fear of fatherhood stems from the fact that we have no point of reference with which to understand this curious little critter who will soon dominate our lives. Throughout my son's first year, I found myself often comparing him to two other entities with which virtually all men are intimately familiar (sometimes disturbingly so): pets and college roommates. Hopefully the following chart will help you understand these similarities and help you begin to understand your future offspring.

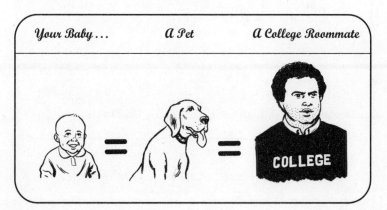

Your Baby . . . *A Pet* *A College Roommate*

(continued)

Your Baby . . .	*A Pet*	*A College Roommate*
is always happy to see you.	✓ (dogs only, of course)	✓ (especially when you can spot him a C-note for a sure thing at the track)
is great to snuggle with in bed.	✓ (would be even better if they made doggie Beano)	✓ (only happened that once, and we shall never speak of it again)
relieves himself whenever and wherever he likes.	✓ (cats make you think you've got them trained, then, when you least expect it . . .	✓ (also known to preserve such moments in pictures)
will pass over a new toy for the box it came in.	✓ (will often occupy the box when the baby's not looking)	✓ (never hit on girlfriend, but always coveted her clothes)
will throw up, and then go right back to eating.	✓ (what is it with cats and plants?)	✓ (ah, spring break)
loves your cutting-edge techie gadgets.	✓ (I'm typing around the cat right now)	✓ (that bastard still has my Commodore 64)

Your Baby...	A Pet	A College Roommate
is amused by all bodily functions.	☑ (not certain, but the dog does seem awfully smug when I scoop his poop)	☑ (photos don't lie)
makes you behave like an idiot.	☑ (see poop-scooping, above)	☑ (can't believe the dean wouldn't buy the "double-dog dare" defense)
makes your life worth living.	☑ (more specifically, the cats seem to believe I was put on this earth just to serve them)	☑ (I, at least, have to live long enough to get that $100 and my Commodore 64 back)

INTERESTING "FACTS" YOU CAN SAY YOU READ IN A BOOK

There is so much data flying around the parenting universe that you could probably find studies that draw contradictory conclusions on just about any topic. You'll frequently hear parents say to each other "I read in a book somewhere . . ." and cite some study to prove that they're not totally incompetent.

So, to help you out, I had the eggheads over at our Department of Logistical and Statistical Obfuscation come up with a list of items with no empirical basis but that, nonetheless, may come in handy if you can recite them convincingly enough. Just preface each claim with "I read it in a book somewhere," which would be completely true.

Brain scan studies have shown that areas of higher functioning in newborn brains become active when they are held by fathers whose breath smells of cigars, gin, and olives.

Recent research strongly suggests that the daily driving of late-model German roadsters with 3.0-liter dual overhead cam, 24-valve inline 255-horsepower engines significantly increases male potency, the likelihood of female children, and wedding-anniversary remembrance.

A longitudinal study has found that college students whose mothers changed most of their diapers when they were babies tend to call home more frequently than those whose fathers changed them more.

Studies have shown that women who drink during pregnancy pose a serious risk to their fetuses, while husbands who drink do nothing but good for all concerned.

Research suggests that fathers who experience a sudden dropoff of golfing and gambling showed a marked increase in nocturnal flatulence, movie quoting, and spontaneous yodeling, whereas increased golfing and gambling led to heightened interest in baking, snuggling, and mothers-in-law.

A series of studies on postpartum metabolism have shown that no single workout burns calories, tautens tummies, and lengthens legs more effectively than waking from a sound sleep, getting out of bed, lifting a baby, changing and/or feeding said baby, replacing baby, and returning to bed. The optimum frequency was found to be six to ten repetitions in an eight-hour period.

Observational research has revealed that when a baby's mother isn't around and that baby is looked after by his or her father, the baby never cries, eats perfectly, and certainly never chews on power cords or bathes in the toilet.

GREAT EXPECTATIONS

*She's Pregnant, So Why
Are You Nauseous?*

Have you ever asked a women when she was due, only to find out in no uncertain terms that she wasn't pregnant? It's not a mistake you make twice. You were just trying to be nice, and it blew up in your face. You felt like an idiot. Well, my friends, deride yourselves no longer. For, as you will discover soon enough, pregnancy is a rich, astonishing, thoroughly bewildering process on any number of levels, and you can't possibly be expected to understand it. Let's face it, for a gender that can't even comprehend simple concepts like snuggling or napkins, don't we men deserve a little latitude when it comes to a complex phenomenon like pregnancy?

Here's an example of just how treacherous the seas of pregnancy can be. You may not have thought about this yet (I certainly hadn't when my wife first became pregnant), but women don't instantaneously transform from their prepregnancy shapes into that distended, waddling figure you'll eventually and disconcertingly find attractive. It takes weeks and weeks, and during that time you'll undoubtedly be asked a familiar yet unexpected question: Do I look fat? That's right, the dreaded question you've struggled for years to answer just got even more complicated. Before the pregnancy, this tricky little question meant your wife was feeling fat. Now it means she doesn't feel fat enough. Confused? You ain't seen nothing yet. Welcome to the wonderful world of pregnancy.

HOW TO REACT TO THE NEWS

Difficulty   *Reward*

My boys can swim!
—GEORGE COSTANZA (JASON ALEXANDER), *SEINFELD*

Before my wife became pregnant, I learned everything I knew about how men were supposed to react from television. Every time I saw some guy's reaction to receiving the news, either on a sitcom or the evening news, they always seemed to take it way too well. They actually seemed happy, and even considered themselves lucky and/or blessed. I wouldn't have used those exact words to describe their state, but rather a somewhat different term of art, which, ironically, is also the act that got them into this mess in the first place. I was pretty sure that when I found out my wife was pregnant, my reaction would most definitely *not* have been suitable for television viewing, and probably could even teach David Mamet a few choice new words.

Having never lived through it before, I naturally assumed that the experience of finding out we were pregnant (see "What You Mean *We*, Woman?" below) would be overwhelmingly traumatic, like when I found out that they'd canceled *Stacked*. All of my fears and insecurities would come crashing down upon me in that single instant as I held in my trembling grasp a small plastic device that my wife had peed upon only moments before. To make matters worse, my wife would stand there expecting me to react instantaneously and without reservation, expressing my profound joy, coupled with a genuinely sweet vulnerability. I was pretty sure that with all that pressure on me I was more likely to throw up, pass out, or glaze over like an Easter ham. I was definitely sure I would not express anything even remotely similar to joy. In fact, there's little chance any joy that I might have felt would be able to get through the shroud of terror that would rapidly envelope my very soul.

And yet, when the moment did come and I looked down at that little pee-drizzled harbinger, my only reaction was, "That is so cool." I neither jumped for joy nor ran for the hills. I didn't think about the consequences, the diapers, the crying, and all the rest, nor could I imagine the happiness that this moment would foretell. For once I was just living in the moment, to the exclusion of all that other stuff, which in itself is an indication of just how amazing that moment can be.

You probably won't freak out either, nor will you definitely be overjoyed, but I can pretty much guarantee that there will be some sense of awe at what you've just done. Conception is at once both fundamentally natural and unfathomably profound. I wouldn't call it a miracle, because I think it's much more complex and intimate than that. But it does feel like you've just achieved something of a higher order than anything you've done before, and you should bask in that glow for as long as you can. In a very short time you'll begin to think of that little creature in there not as a marvel of nature but as a parasite, and you probably won't think otherwise until he graduates from college. So for now let's figure out a few ways to help you make sure you can appreciate that moment before reality comes crashing in.

Forget the Future

As you'll see throughout this book, there are many moments during your journey to fatherhood that never turn out quite the way you think they will. You think you might pass out during delivery, but when you're in that delivery room experiencing it right then and there, it's a totally different thing, and you make it through. You think your daily routine as a father will be completely laborious and dreadful, but it turns out differently. You can't imagine how you'll be happy as a father, but when you actually are a father your life has a way of finding its equilibrium. All of these moments illustrate the fact that anticipation is not reality, and there are countless such moments on the path to fatherhood. The more you can resist the urge to think ahead about how things *might* go and how you *may* react, the more you can appreciate the reality when you're actually in it. So, with regard to getting "the news," rather than worrying about it, try waiting for the moment to come and see how you react. I realize that this is much easier said than done, since it's not something that comes naturally to men. But there are things you can do to increase your chances.

Focus

Pregnancy is about so many things. It's about the future and everything that comes along with it, from the mundane to the majestic. It sets in motion an epic undertaking so vast and all-encompassing that it's made stronger men than me sob like a disgraced televangelist. It's all too easy to jump way ahead and start thinking about your child's life and forget that it all started when two cells merged and then started dividing.

I would definitely recommend that while you still have the unoccupied brain capacity, you learn a bit about the biology of reproduction. *National Geographic* recently produced a fascinating video called *In the Womb*. You should check it out before you try to get pregnant. Then, when your wife finally does get pregnant, you'll be able to appreciate the amazing things that are happening right then, without jumping ahead and starting to worry about preschools.

Feel

I realize that feelings are almost exclusively a female domain, but this is one time when you should really try your best to pay attention to what you're actually feeling. One of the reasons I was so anxious about getting the news was that I felt there was one particular way that I was supposed to feel about it. In reality, the only way I *could* feel about the news was the way that I *actually* felt about it. I would have rather just let it happen and see how I felt, rather than gauging my reaction relative to some societal—or worse yet, sitcom—ideal.

Ultimately, if you're true to your feelings, it doesn't matter how you react when you get the news. You'll definitely have a mix of feelings, and I'm sure your wife will as well. If you are genuinely happy, that will certainly help ease her fears. If you freak out, either her nurturing instincts will kick in or she'll get to release some stress smacking you upside the head. Regardless of what happens, you'll both look back on this moment fondly, and if you did freak out, you'll also have a good laugh.

What You Mean *We,* Woman?

You may have noticed a slight but highly suggestive change in the way pregnancy is described of late. Rather than saying "She's pregnant," you'll hear people saying, "We're pregnant." I'm not sure exactly what prompted this semantic shift, but I can guarantee it wasn't a guy who thought it up. Even the most masochistic father-to-be wouldn't wish that particular scourge upon himself, although after the child is born some men delude themselves into feelings of jealousy regarding the experience that their wives had during childbirth. To those guys I say: You want to feel pain? Cultivate a massive kidney stone or take a kickball to the groin. Otherwise, consider yourself lucky, and stop trying to ruin it for everyone else.

The switch from "she" to "we" is more likely a plot among the women, with a few possible goals. It could be that women want to instill a greater sense of solidarity with their husbands. This is a risky strategy, as men may take their sympathy a bit too far. If women thought a healthy husband was useless, just wait until they have to deal with a husband stricken with morning sickness (see

Think you're missing out on labor pains? Try kidney stones (left) or a kickball to the groin (right).

"How to Avoid Sympathy Pains"). Or it may be that women want their husbands to feel pregnant and pack on a few pounds so that as the pregnancy develops they won't seem so enormous by comparison.

Now that I think about it, neither of these scenarios seems particularly bad for guys. Sure, you may throw up a bit, but you'll score major sympathy points from the wife and you'll seem like a perfect husband to everyone else. Besides that, it gives you the green light to eat whatever you want and let yourself go for nine months. Given how good a deal men seem to get from this new terminology, I'm now beginning to think it couldn't actually have been a woman who introduced it. It's hard to believe that women would embrace something that ultimately works against them. It must have been introduced by someone adept at convincing people to espouse beliefs that directly counter their own self-interests, a master of doublespeak who could capitalize on people's fears and manipulate them to do his bidding with total disregard for their well-being. I'll bet it was Karl Rove in drag.

Finally, after the dust settles and you've told your parents and everyone else the good news, you should take a moment to think about what you just went through. Looking back, you will hardly be able to imagine what you were worried about. As you move through pregnancy and into fatherhood, you'll encounter many such moments, and they all follow pretty much this same pattern. So the next time you start to worry about how things will be sometime in the future, remember this first episode, relax, and let the moment come to you. You'll do fine.

SEVEN THINGS TO DO THE MOMENT YOU FIND OUT SHE'S PREGNANT

1. Start Saving Old Cell Phones, PDAs, and MP3 Players

Babies have an innate attraction to anything you want them to stay away from, and they're particularly drawn to all things high-tech. In fact, if you were to line up a dozen different objects, ranging from a wood block to a cell phone, most babies would indicate their preference for the phone by drooling on, dropping, and otherwise defiling it much more enthusiastically than all the others.

Luckily, a little forethought can save you the indignity of pleading with the customer service guy at Circuit City that "drool-related malfunctions" should be covered under the warranty. Seeing that most high-tech gadgets are obsolete only minutes after you buy them, you're always on the lookout for a good excuse to upgrade. Knowing that your baby is going to destroy any cell phone, PDA, or MP3 player within a six-foot radius, wouldn't you rather he go after last week's model and leave your new one alone? To make it happen, start saving all your old devices and introduce them to the baby one at a time. Unfortunately, your baby will grow tired of his current model about as quickly as you did, so make sure you've got a newer version stashed away to keep him away from your own.

2. Bank Your Sick Days

No matter how healthy you've been to this point, a baby will knock you on your ass faster than Tijuana tap water. Before I became a father, I had gotten sick no more than once a year. By the time my son was a year old, I'd had no fewer than four debilitating illnesses, each one memorable in its own god-awful way. For example, when the stomach bug hit our house I was privileged to experience "The Helicopter"* for the first time since college. Someday I'll have to return the favor, probably by "accidentally" showing his first girlfriend every nude photo and video we've ever taken of him. (Just to be prepared, I'd better drop a few bills into the Therapy Jar.)

3. Start Saving for College

If *CSI* has taught me anything, it's that you can't take out a large insurance policy on yourself and then fake your own death to pay for your children's education. So, we'll have to move on to Plan B.

A year of private college these days can easily cost over $30,000. If we project out over the next eighteen years, when your child will be starting his freshman year, my rough calculations indicate that the cost will be somewhere around half a million dollars a year. Okay, I may be exaggerating a bit, but I wanted to lighten the mood before I gave you the correct figures. Realistically—you might want to sit down for this—the total cost for a year of college will be gut-wrenchingly close to $100,000. Multiply that by four (or five or six, depending on your genes) and you'll be near or beyond that half-million-dollar mark. It sounds pretty daunting, I know, but don't forget that wages will go up as well. Although if the average parents' wages increase as

---

*To put it delicately, imagine a scenario while seated in the bathroom in which imminent eruptions from certain multiple orifices would prompt you to spin around quickly, thus emulating a helicopter.

anemically over the next twenty years as they did over the past twenty, that $100K is going to loom pretty much just as large then as it does now. You may want to consider investing in a Baby Bowflex and hope that the kid gets a free ride on the jock docket.

Actually, there are lots of scholarship and financial aid opportunities. Sure, twenty years from now you'll probably be getting your aid from the governments of China or India, but who better to help you out, since in all likelihood your kid will just be training to do tech support for Chinese and Indian companies anyway?

Seriously, though, the more money you can put aside now, the easier it will be to meet your financial goals when he's ready to start school. For example, if you planned on paying half of your child's expenses, you would need to start saving about $300 per month (assuming an average 7 percent annual growth on your investment). I realize that's some major scratch, but if you wait until he's ten years old, the monthly investment jumps to almost $900! All that being said, I'd recommend not getting too hung up on the specific numbers; after all these estimates are for the most expensive schools. Just try to start saving as much as you can.

4. Get in the Information Loop

There is an unfathomable amount of information that you and your wife (mostly your wife) will learn over the next couple of months. Many guys find it so overwhelming that they just bury their heads and hope to get by on their looks (bad idea). One way to keep up with the basic information about the pregnancy's progress is to sign up for the "My Baby This Week" e-mail newsletter at babycenter.com. They've also got lots of good information from other dads-to-be.

5. Stake Your Claim

As I'll describe below in "How to Be Useful," there are certain tasks that will need to be done for which your masculine talents are perfectly suited. You should jump on them from the start. Not only will that get you involved in the whole process, but it can help you get out of doing some of the more repugnant tasks. There might be a new car to be bought, new techie gear to be researched, and plenty of new furniture and accessories to be assembled. If you eagerly embrace these tasks, your wife may finally see that these things are simply more suited to the masculine mind. Even if she doesn't, what do you care? As long as you don't have to decide which diaper rash cream is the best, all is well. (Actually, that's an easy one. The list begins and ends with Boudreaux's Butt Paste.)

6. Offhand Remarks

Improving your off-hand dexterity might help your basketball game, but it will definitely make parenting easier. In particular, you'll find there are times when you're holding the baby and you just can't eat with your dominant hand or use the phone on your normal side. So I'd suggest that you start working on your off hand as soon as possible. To create as accurate a simulation as possible, you may want to try eating or talking on the phone with one hand while holding a rabid badger with the other.

7. From Here to Paternity

As soon as possible, start looking into how much time you can get away from work when the baby is born. The Family and Medical Leave Act (FMLA) mandates that employees get twelve weeks of unpaid leave for the birth or adoption of a baby (although there are some exceptions). Check with your human resources department, or visit the Department of Labor's Web site at www.dol.gov for more information.

Everyone tells you how important it is to spend as much time as possible with the new baby, but many guys can find it difficult to do so. Some may not be able to afford an extended unpaid leave, while others may feel that taking all that time off will hurt their careers. Many men believe that they won't have much of an impact on the baby during these early months. In fact, if I didn't have the flexibility in my career to easily take the time off, I definitely wouldn't have spent so much time with my son during his first few months. I had no idea how much I would appreciate being able to bond with my son and watch him develop every single day. It's a unique time in a baby's life, and it doesn't last very long at all. So trust me, and do whatever you can to spend as much time as you can possibly afford with your new baby. You won't regret it.

HOW TO BE USELESS

Difficulty **Reward**

Most pregnancies appear to get under way with relatively equal participation by both parties involved. Of course, if we look closely at what actually happens (on a microscopic level, not merely what you can see with a Bushnell Voyager Series 60 mm Refractor Telescope coincidentally directed toward an open bedroom window some ninety-five feet directly across the street), it's anything but equal. The egg involved is among the most complex cells in all of nature, waiting passively and disinterestedly while thousands of sperm, basically just frantic little blobs of DNA with tails, flail around trying to make an impression. Sounds a lot like high school, actually. From that moment forward, it's pretty much all up to her.

That means that the true extent of men's necessary involvement in the whole pregnancy is limited to those ninety minutes of procreative intercourse (I understand that other men may finish more quickly, but that's nothing to be ashamed of). Beyond that, there's very little we can actually do to directly participate in the pregnancy. We must, though, make ourselves useful by learning how to be useless.

For millions of years, we guys thrived on usefulness (or at least creating the illusion of usefulness). Our caveman ancestors went and hunted down a mastodon when the family would've been happy with beetles, bark, and the occasional cute little bunny rabbit. Modern man will change a flat tire all by himself in the pouring rain, despite the AAA card that bulks up his wallet and makes his butt numb.

We're ambitious go-getters by nature. I know this may not be apparent on any given wintry NFL Sunday, when many of our brethren spread out supine with a frosty cold one propped atop our ample guts as we struggle to reach the remote just beyond our pudgy grasp. But it's true. Beneath that vintage Oakland Raiders jersey, dabbed ever so sweetly with Durkee's RedHot Sauce, beats the slightly gristly heart of a champion. It's why we never back down from a challenge. It's why we never rest until the job is completed. It's also why we occasionally let a Samsung 5200 BTU air conditioner drop from a second-story window, sending it crashing to the sidewalk below (or so I've heard). And, of course, it's why we flail about like a white guy at '80s Night when there's a problem we can't do anything about.

Pregnancy and fatherhood are filled with countless such problems that are beyond even our copious, scary talents. The sooner you learn to handle yourself in these situations, the less likely your wife is to go Denise Richards on your sorry ass and make a break for the exit.

Here's a scenario you'll probably experience: Your wife is a few months pregnant, and imperceptible to you, her favorite jeans are getting a tad snug. She spots Jessica Simpson's bare midriff in a supermarket tabloid, starts sobbing pitifully, and rips open the Nutter Butters. You tense up, embarrassed, and ask her what's wrong, and she shoots you a searing glare of red-hot death. "Your demon seed has sullied my soul, that's what's wrong," she'll say, or something to that effect, and you begin to get the sense that you may have misspoken.

The only way to prevent such incidents from becoming daily occurrences is to do the one thing that comes least naturally to us: nothing. In these cases, the best strategy is to just be supportive (I know it sounds ridiculous, but it's true). From the moment you even think of having kids, you must prepare yourself to sympathize with every mood swing, hold her hair during every predawn retch, breathe along with every contraction, and shed a tear for every overworked nipple. (Hers, not yours. I hope.) For a gender much more comfortable hammering, chopping, and exploding stuff, this kind of "soft labor" (a.k.a. "wuss work") is a lot harder than it sounds.

Luckily for us, expectations are set snake-belly low. Our

ultimate goal isn't to solve all her problems and make her as perky as a cheerleader hopped up on Red Bull; it's just to not make a bad situation worse. Your wife is not broken, and they sure as hell don't sell anything at Home Depot that can fix her, so you've got to spring into inaction and "just be supportive." She's in a very precarious situation, so choose your words (and deeds) carefully. Here's a quick little primer to help you through some of the stickier situations:

> Don't ask, "What can I do to help?"
> Instead suggest, "Please let me know if there's anything I
> can do for you."
>
> Don't start kneading her shoulders and rubbing her back.
> Instead just take her hand and let her guide you to do
> what's best.
>
> And, in the name of all that's holy, don't try tough love and
> tell her to snap out of it (unless you don't mind a gene-
> splicing knee to the groin).
> Tell her you love her and you're always there whenever she
> needs you. (Even if it sounds ridiculously corny to you,
> it most likely won't to her. And if it does, odds are
> you'll give her a good laugh, which definitely counts as
> a win.)

Over time, she'll gently guide you in the right direction, with a helpful suggestion here and a bitch-slap there. Just remember, she's probably pretty scared, completely exhausted, and riddled with mind- and body-altering hormones. So be a man, and for once in your life muster up the courage to be useless.

Don't Go There

Unfortunately, being supportive can only get you so far. You may need to try something with which most guys have little or no experience: empathy. From morning sickness and cravings all the way through to contractions and delivery, I found it very difficult to really appreciate how tough the whole ordeal could be. Sure, I felt bad for my wife at times, but mostly I was just glad it wasn't happening to me. If you feel this way, do yourself a favor and keep it to yourself. Do not give your wife any indication that you're anything less than fully engaged in every sensation she experiences.

For example, here's one common mistake that I made (and I know at least a few other people, including my brother, who made the same mistake). About five or six months into the pregnancy, you'll be amazed to realize that you're five or six months into the pregnancy. The time really does seem to go by quickly, but I'm reasonably confident your wife will not feel the same way. I was stupid enough to express this sentiment in front of my wife, who promptly let me know in no uncertain terms that I would pay dearly for my transgression. And while I would rather change every diaper and do every nighttime feeding rather than experience pregnancy and delivery firsthand, I still feel kind of bad.

HOW TO BE USEFUL

 Difficulty   Reward

Eighty percent of success is showing up.
—WOODY ALLEN

There are times during the pregnancy when you'll actually be called upon to do stuff. Ironically enough, you'll probably find it easier to be useful during the pregnancy than to be useless. Very little is really expected of you, you can usually pick and choose what you want to do, and there are several tasks that clearly fall within the manly domain.

The T-Ball Scenario

Being a good husband during pregnancy is like playing T-ball. Given how low the expectations are, you'd really have to work at it to fail. Even as husbands are expected to participate more and more in the process, society still diminishes our role during pregnancy to the extent that just remaining conscious throughout the whole process (see "How to Remain Conscious During Delivery") is considered an acceptable contribution. That being said, would it kill you to put in a little (very little) extra effort for your baby's mama?

The best thing you can do early on is to express interest in the whole pregnancy adventure. Your wife will instantly embark on an epic journey to gather any and all information about what she's going through, so the least you can do is tag along. I'm not suggesting that you have to read every book she brings home, but at least skim through most of them. Here's an insider tip that will not only show her how interested you are, but will also make sure she avoids reading a book that will make her totally paranoid (and make you totally miserable):

The single best-selling pregnancy book of all time is *What to Expect When You're Expecting*. Your wife will no doubt receive or buy a copy at some point. Under no circumstances should you allow her to read it. While this book is very informative, it also includes every possible nightmare scenario about what can come to pass during a pregnancy. It will turn your wife into a complete basket case. Instead, make sure she has *The Girlfriends' Guide to Pregnancy* by Vicki Iovine. This book is just as informative, much more reasonable, and really funny. Getting this book for your wife shows her just how cued in you are to her needs, and will also save you from consoling her during any number of sobbing fits brought on by that other book.

Next, agree to go to every class she proposes and try your best to make it to every doctor's appointment. Not only is it important to support her during these anxious times, but it also prevents her from getting an inexorable upper hand on everything baby-related moving forward. Think about it: suppose she suggests you both take a class on breastfeeding, and you immediately take on any and all new projects at work with the goal of staying in the office every waking hour of every day. Now, picture her at the class, surrounded by pregnant women with their loving husbands, sharing a knowing and furious glance with every woman there. The class gives your wife several hours to stew over exactly how and to what extent she's going to make you pay.

In particular, be sure to agree to attend a birthing class. These classes are so helpful for men that you really should make sure to find one to take, even if your wife doesn't do so first. Not only is it truly amazing to learn what's going on inside your wife's body, but the more you know about the realities of delivery, the better prepared you'll be to both help your wife through it and not lose your lunch in the process.

Easy Pickings
There are a daunting number of things to do before the baby arrives. Luckily, you've got almost nine months to get them all

done. To guarantee that you are assigned the least distasteful of these tasks, I recommend that you stake your claim to the better ones early on. It's kind of like back in college, when everyone stood in line to pick classes. If only you hadn't overslept, you would have gotten "History of Rock: The Zeppelin Years" instead of "Intro to the Cohomology of Simplectic Manifolds."

Face it: you're going to have to do these things anyway, so you might as well appear to do them eagerly. Plus, once you've got your pet projects, you can always rely on them to get out of the more odious tasks that will come along. For example, at some point you'll need to go to one of the baby superstores to stock up on shockingly expensive "essential" items. You can, coincidentally, schedule minivan test drives that day (no harm in taking their latest roadster out for a spin as well while you're there), or if you have to go to the store, you can focus your energies on talking to a salesperson about crib assembly or the latest in baby monitor technology instead of just listening in on the great nipple shield debate.

Be the Man

As I mentioned above, you're better off picking which tasks you want to do early on in the process. But which ones should you pick? As you will soon realize, many of the tasks involved in baby preparation are just perfect for men. For example, if you're going to buy a new minivan, forget for the moment that it's a minivan, and instead focus on the fact that it's a new car. You should jump at the chance to be in charge of the research for that purchase. You can get online and dig through all consumer ratings, check out prices, and haggle with the local dealers. Plus, as we'll see in "How to Feel Manly in a Minivan," you can totally trick it out with any and all available options, no matter how ridiculous your wife may think they are.

Besides the car purchase, there are other types of tasks perfectly suited to your masculine talents. There are new high-tech gadgets to be researched and purchased. These include baby monitors, digital cameras and camcorders, software for editing all those photos and videos, CD/DVD burners for archiving everything, and so on. Plus there are lots of peripheral items that you could make an argument for, such as new cell phones and a DVR. Next time you go to Circuit City or Best Buy, take a look around; I'm sure you could find even more purchases that could be justified in the name of paternal love.

Finally, there are the finances. If you enjoy dealing with money matters at all, or if you just don't want your wife to get involved, take care of the college savings plans, bank accounts, life insurance, medical savings accounts, and anything else that might come up.

Unfortunately, your wife may interpret your enthusiasm for these matters as a general regard for all things baby, and come to expect your involvement in every last detail. To you unfortunate souls I offer my apologies, and this consoling refrain: "So don't forget, folks, that's what you get, folks, for makin' whoopee."

HOW TO HELP HER GET OFF THE SAUCE

Difficulty   *Reward*

Obviously, pregnant women should stop smoking and drinking completely, and minimize their caffeine consumption. The real question is, to what extent do fathers need to do the same? I would recommend that you follow the same restrictions as she does, although not necessarily for the reasons you might expect.

Smoking

There's no question that if you're a smoker, you should quit the moment you and your wife even consider having a baby. You should do this not only because it's a nasty habit and potentially very harmful to the developing fetus, but for reasons of self-preservation as well. After the baby arrives, you're going to need all the lung capacity you can muster to hold your breath during those particularly evil diaper changes (see "How to Change Diapers: The Taming of the Poo"), and the pleasure you get from smoking now could result in much greater disgust down the road.

Drinking

I would also recommend that you join her in cutting out alcohol, or at least cutting back. Sure, it will make her feel as if you're really participating in the pregnancy if you give up your precious spirits, but once again there is a selfish motive to hopping on the wagon (or at least jogging alongside it for a while): to lower your tolerance, thus increasing the wallop alcohol will provide when you really need it. For example, when the baby's just stopped crying after countless hours and your head's about to explode, you'll really appreciate the instantaneous, stupefying intoxication afforded the teetotaler. By the way, if you have any difficult limiting or eliminating your alcohol consumption, now's the time to get help. If you've got a drinking problem now, you're going to be in big trouble once the baby arrives.

To help you along the path to temporary sobriety, let's find a few passable substitutes. I found that my wife usually craved foods from her childhood, so when it came time to think about drinks she could have, I started with an old classic we all remember from when we were kids: the Shirley Temple. From there, I started making other nonalcoholic drinks, and it helped us both stay dry. Plus, for many of them, once the baby arrived all we had to do was add some booze and we were good to go. Here are some of the recipes we used, which I hope can tide you over until the baby arrives.

Virgin Cocktails
(Note the irony)

THE SHIRLEY TEMPLE

Despite the fact that you may only know this drink from your childhood—when you bellied up to the bar and stood on your tiptoes to reach a tumbler of this pale red, fizzy concoction, complete with modified cherrylike garnish—it's not half bad. Plus it's got a nostalgic, lighthearted vibe to it, which can be helpful when the labors of pregnancy grow burdensome.

By the way, as if this drink's ingredients and name wouldn't embarrass any self-respecting guy who might order it, its original name was a "Pussyfoot."

5–6 ounces ginger ale   Maraschino cherry
Splash of grenadine

Add ginger ale, grenadine, and ice to a tumbler or highball glass. Stir gently and garnish with the cherry.

Optional: You can also add a splash of orange juice and an orange slice garnish.

VIRGIN MARGARITA

Since lots of pregnant women crave both salt and ice, blending this drink and rimming the glass with salt could be a real winner with the wife. But be sure to ask first, since she may be going through a phase where even the thought of such things will turn her stomach.

Half of a 6-ounce can of
    frozen lemonade
Half of a 6-ounce can of
    frozen limeade
1–2 cups crushed ice

1/2 cup club soda
Coarse salt
1/2 cup orange juice
Lime wedges

Combine the lemonade, limeade, ice, orange juice, and club soda in a blender. Mix on High until thoroughly blended.

Pour enough salt onto a small plate to coat the bottom. Rub the rims of margarita or cocktail glasses with the lime wedges, then invert the glasses and dip the rims into the salt.

Pour the mixture into the glasses and garnish with the lime wedges.

VIRGIN COSMOPOLITAN

2 ounces cranberry juice
1 ounce sparkling water

1 ounce orange juice
Splash of lime juice

Combine ingredients in a shaker over ice. Shake and strain into a martini glass. Garnish with a twist of lime.

VIRGIN MARTINI

If you're just desperate to experience the cool, clean perfection of a martini, here's all you can do: Chill a martini glass. Add one or three olives, and enjoy. You could also make a Virgin Appletini, which is just apple juice in a martini glass, garnished with a twist of lemon.

Caffeine

The jury is still out regarding the effect of caffeine on fetal development, but most women are encouraged to limit their consumption, with the understanding that too much caffeine can't possibly be good. As with alcohol, I suggest eliminating caffeine both out of commiseration with your wife and out of sheer self-interest. Once the baby arrives, you're regularly going to need as much of a caffeine jolt as you can get. When you've got an early meeting and need to create the illusion of sentience, or when you just want to go crazy and stay up past eight o'clock on a Saturday night, you'll want access to the kick that only caffeine offers to the uninitiated.

Quitting caffeine can be a miserable process, marked most notably by irritability, fatigue, and headaches that could drop a rhino. The best way to avoid serious withdrawal symptoms is to step down your consumption gradually. So if you regularly drink four cups of coffee a day, start by replacing one cup a day with half regular and half decaf. If that works out, go up to two cups regular and two cups half and half. From there, just keep shifting to lower-caffeine drinks. You can shift down from the half-caff drinks to tea, which has on average half the caffeine of regular coffee. Then go down to decaf, which has very little caffeine, and finally to herbal tea. If you find that you have bad headaches along the way, you can take aspirin or another headache medication. Just keep in mind that many of these contain caffeine, which kind of defeats the purpose.

Good luck, and if you ever need inspiration to continue trying to quit, just think about how great it will be to drink again when you're a daddy and you really deserve it.

HEAD ON DOWN TO THE BIG QUEASY

How to Deal with Morning Sickness

Difficulty 🍼🍼🍼🍼   *Reward* 🍺

Just how bad is morning sickness? Years after their babies are born, many women remember the discomfort of morning sickness more clearly than the pain of delivery. *That's* bad. Ever been seasick? Ever eat a tainted burrito? Ever watched *The View*? I'm pretty sure morning sickness is like all of those combined, every day for weeks!

You might think that morning sickness is just nature's way of getting men to do more chores, but there actually is a legitimate purpose for it (or at least there used to be a legitimate purpose for it). Early on in pregnancy, the fetus is particularly susceptible to many toxins that the mother may ingest. Bitter foods, like broccoli, are particularly high in such toxins, and their consumption should be minimized during this time. In the days before early pregnancy tests, debilitating nausea was a surefire way to alert women to their condition and keep them from eating strong-tasting, bitter foods. It also stopped them from doing overly strenuous activity, which helped protect the fetus. It's a pretty straightforward Darwinian explanation. On the other hand, if you believe in a higher power, morning sickness is conclusive proof that God is a guy.

As someone at least partially responsible for your wife's current state of misery, you're obligated to provide some aid and comfort. The big question is: What exactly should you do? Basically, it all comes down to communication. You've got to talk to your wife in advance about it, and figure out in detail how she wants you to help. For example:

1. To Help or Not to Help

My wife is a puker; she always has been. When she'd get sick from binge drinking (if you can call half a cosmopolitan a binge), it was clear that she didn't want me there to hold her hair back or deliver a courtesy flush. So when the morning sickness began, I assumed that the same rules applied. I was wrong. And although I felt terrible hearing those pitiful heaves, as I later found out, I didn't feel nearly as bad as she felt all by herself in there. We worked it out eventually, but make sure you know up front what she wants you to do.

2. Go Public

There will be many times when you'll have to cover for your wife, who has run off to the bathroom or the bushes. You'll need to keep in mind that there are different levels of security clearance for different people. There are those with complete clearance, who already know she's pregnant and to whom the toilet-hugging details can be fully revealed. Others may only have partial clearance, while still others are to be kept in the dark. Find out from her how she wants you to handle it. Should you avoid the truth? Or if you tell the truth, should you downplay it as nothing significant, or does she want to play the sympathy card?

3. Tell It Like It Is

Many women are frustrated, confused, and even scared by what's going on with their bodies. You are a ready and easy target, and she may take out her fears and frustrations on you. It's also possible, given all the changes she's experiencing, that you might be unwittingly contributing to her symptoms (see "The Sense of a Woman," below). You need to make sure she tells you everything you need to know to help her get through this. As little intuition as you had about your wife when she was normal, you've got even less in her current state. Make sure she brings you up to speed.

The Sense of a Woman

Among the many bizarre physiological transformations your wife may go through during her pregnancy, this one may be the strangest: her sense of smell is likely to heighten dramatically, and certain previously acceptable smells may become totally repulsive. This change tends to happen early in the pregnancy—most likely due to a spike in estrogen—and can be a rather abrupt initiation for husbands to the wacky world of pregnancy. As with the nausea and vomiting, there probably once were evolutionary advantages to this change. These days, though, it's just weird.

Allow me to share the story of how I came to experience this peculiar malady. I was innocently going about my own business, having just finished inhaling an Italian hoagie with extra hot peppers. My wife told me she didn't feel too well, so I gave her a big hug and told her I loved her, and she vomited on my shoes. She pushed me away, gasping for air, and told me in no uncertain terms that my breath reeked like a hamper backstage at *Fear Factor*. I felt terrible, so I popped a Halls and told her I loved her, and she vomited on my socks, proclaiming the evils of mentho-lyptus between heaves.

Having assessed the situation tactically, and wanting desperately to keep my bare feet vomit-free, I immediately sprang into action: I got the hell out of the house before the hoagie worked its way through, drove over to Costco, and got myself a nine-month supply of Beano.

Finally, the supreme irony of morning sickness is that with all that puking going on, your wife is likely to leave the toilet seat up all the time. And late one night, you may learn firsthand why she's been bugging you to put the seat down all these years.

HOW TO LEARN EVERYTHING YOU NEED TO KNOW (IN NINE MONTHS OR LESS)

Difficulty   Reward

Then there's the dyptheria-tetanus, what they call
the dip-tet. You gotta get 'em dip-tet boosters yearly
or they'll develop lockjaw and night vision.

—DOT (FRANCES MCDORMAND), *RAISING ARIZONA*

Before I became a parent, the single greatest mystery to me, besides how anyone could be happy about having twins (see "How to React to the News"), was this: How do parents learn all the stuff that they need to know about parenting? How do they find out which diapers they prefer, when the baby should be sleeping, which car seat to get, and a million other things? Not only was I totally intimidated by the volume of knowledge that I thought I need to attain, I had no idea where it all came from. Even now, when I'm on the other side and I've already learned a ridiculous amount of information about parenting, it still remains somewhat of a mystery as to just how I acquired that knowledge. The difference is that before fatherhood I was totally freaked out by my own ignorance and I worked hard to overcome it. Now I'm completely confident that I'll know what I need to know when I need to know it, and I just sit back and let it come to me.

You may think that I'm about to answer all of those questions for you. You would be wrong. Not only will I not strive to answer all of them, I'm going to make a concerted effort not to answer any of them. If you do happen to get an answer to a basic parenting question from this book, I assure you, it got in here purely by accident. What I will do is guarantee that all the information is out there and will find its way into your brain.

A Brief Note About Baby Farts

I have a theory about baby farts. At first I couldn't believe that a baby could produce such thunderous flatulence. When my son was just a few weeks old, he'd make a *tuchis* ruckus that could startle a hippo. It defied the laws of physics. If you consider the mechanics of brass instruments, it's clear that the smaller the resonating chamber, the higher the register of the notes played. Thus, a trumpet plays higher notes than a tuba. It follows that a baby's "nether notes" should be much higher than an adult's, but much to my shock, amusement, and occasional jealousy, they're not. My baby boy could rattle the rafters with rear-end rumblings previously ascribed exclusive to his dear old dad. Granted, this came in handy when I sought to deflect blame whenever I found myself falsely (or rightly) accused of having dealt it (see "How to Use the Baby to Get Away with Just About Anything"), but it still left me perplexed.

I inquired with a friend of mine who fancies himself quite an authority on the subject (a claim to which I can, unfortunately, attest). He answered the question as if he'd been waiting his entire adult life to be asked it: "Obviously," he said with the calm resolve of a Zen master imparting the wisdom of the ages to an eager pupil, "babies are so relaxed and uninhibited. That, my friend, is the key." All parents lament the day when their child loses his pure innocence and wonder. Now we can add "sphincteral abandon" to that list of fleeting childhood qualities that will soon be silenced (or at least transposed to a higher register) by the weight of the world.

There are three important things to consider when you get worried about the volume of information you'll need to know.

1. Information Overload

Once you enter the world of pregnancy and parenthood, you become privy to a well of information so vast it makes the *Encyclopedia Brittanica* look like the publically accessible notes from Dick Cheney's energy task force. You will be so inundated with information that just by osmosis you'll find that you suddenly know things and you have no idea where the information came from. You may wonder how that happens. Here's my theory:

The moment you see a positive result on that early pregnancy test, a tiny transponder within the test device itself emits a signal bearing your name and home address to every producer of baby products and the subscription office of every parenting magazine*. Even before the ink dries on the first of many Xanax prescriptions, you'll receive complimentary copies of *Fit Pregnancy, American Baby, Panicky Parents*, and *The Breeder Reader*.

And then there are all the books. There must be thousands of parenting books out there. My goodness, could there possibly be any market more saturated than parenting books? I can't imagine how anyone could be so foolish as to believe that they could add anything to what's already been written. Even more amazing is why any publisher would agree to publish a new parenting book. I would think that they would immediately shred any proposal they received on the subject, following up with an irate phone call to the author along the lines of, "How dare you insult our intelligence and waste the precious resources of the United States

* Not really.

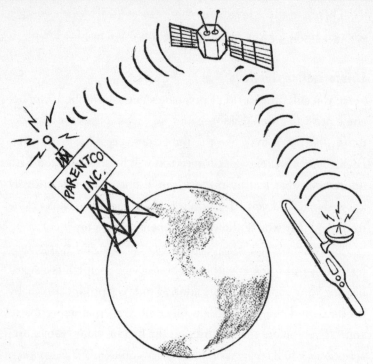

The moment you find out she's pregnant, you're in the system.

Postal Service with such a redundant, unnecessary piece of detritus? We've got a good mind to report you to the local authorities and get you under psychiatric observation, as you must certainly be a threat to yourself and others."

Actually, after a brief consultation with my editor, I've decided to rephrase that last paragraph slightly. Here goes:

And then there are the books. There are many fine books on parenting, published by fine and beneficent publishers, that provide an invaluable resource to the expectant parent. My favorite, and the one I think would be most well received by new fathers, is *The Baby Owner's Manual: Operating Instructions, Trouble-Shooting Tips, and Advice on First-Year Maintenance* from Quirk Books, the people who brought you the Worst-Case Scenario books.

You'll also encounter innumerable teachers along the way. I never even considered this ahead of time, but just about every medical person you meet will tell you what you need to be doing. I always thought pediatricians just checked out the baby the way my doctor does with me. In fact, at every appointment our pediatrician gives us an extensive checklist of foods, medicines, and behavioral suggestions to guide us along our way. Actually, the whole experience has left me wondering if my own primary care doctor would write up one of those cheat sheets for me.

Finally, there are your friends and family. The single best, most fruitful sources of information are other people who have been through the same thing. Just be sure to keep in mind the personality of the person giving the advice. Remember, pregnancy and parenting may change what you do, but they don't change who you are. If your friend was flaky before having kids, he'll probably be a flaky parent.

2. It's a "Need-to-Know" Situation

The most important realization I've had about becoming a well-informed parent is this: you don't need to know everything all at once; you only need to know something when you need to know it. For example, how do you know which diapers you prefer? Before having a baby, you don't even know what criteria to use, let alone which brand performs best. But, as you may infer, diapers become a rather constant presence in your life once the baby arrives. In just a few days you'll have enough firsthand data to perform a complex multivariate regression to discover which is the brand for you. Also note that with this example, as with so many other decisions you make as a parent, it hardly makes any difference which one you choose anyway.

As those of you with an MBA may already have realized, baby knowledge is best accumulated using a Just In Time inventory strategy. That means that you don't need to clutter up your brain with all sorts of knowledge that won't be any good to you for months. Just focus on what you need to know at the moment, and trust that in the next moment, if there's something else you'll need to know, then you'll know it.

It's also worth noting that you don't need to hang onto any knowledge that's no longer necessary. By the time my son was six months old, I had already forgotten vast swaths of information that only a few months before I was worried I'd never be able to know.

By the way, the Just in Time strategy also applies to the vast majority of stuff you'll need for the baby, so don't get too freaked out if you don't feel like your house is completely stocked ahead of time.

Everyone's an Authority

The biggest challenge facing parents-to-be, when they're totally inundated with information (much of it contradictory), is to figure out which advice is worth taking and which should be ignored. Ultimately, you'll recognize that there are very few objective truths in the realm of childrearing, and the most important thing is that you find a way of going about it that works for you. When it comes to reading books and magazines, it's best to heed the words of the great George Orwell: "The best books are those . . . that tell you what you know already."

If a book harps on all the things that could go wrong with your pregnancy or

> gets all preachy about how you should behave, or if a magazine promotes a style of parenting that you're uncomfortable with, just don't read them. As I mentioned above, there are plenty of other sources of information. Keep looking until you find ones that work for you.

3. Go to Trial

You'll immediately learn that parenting, particularly with regard to behavioral issues, is definitely a trial-and-error undertaking. Every child is unique, and there are countless ways in which that uniqueness expresses itself. Regardless of how many books you read or how many questions you ask, you're just going to have to try different things until you find out what works.

HOW TO AVOID SYMPATHY PAINS

Difficulty *Reward*

Throughout her pregnancy, your wife will experience a variety of discomforts, from aches and pains to insomnia, digestive irregularities, nausea, headaches, and much more. And, of course, it all culminates with delivery, which is no walk in the park. It's quite likely that during the nine or so months of pregnancy, you will also experience similar problems. Most of the time it's probably just a coincidence. After all, you'd expect to get a headache when shopping for baby supplies, and you'd have to be completely delusional to not get nauseous thinking about your baby's college education. Sometimes these ailments actually qualify as sympathy pains, and become what is known as couvade (from the French word for "to hatch") syndrome. Whatever you call them—and regardless of whether or not they indicate that you're a total fruitcake—the symptoms, discomfort, and potential for embarrassment are real.

Just how bad can it get? You may have seen that episode of *House* where a patient came into the clinic complaining of nausea and insomnia. Of course, Dr. House handled this delicate matter with his typical sensitivity. He told him that he's got couvade syndrome and he should stop whining. The patient's condition deteriorated to the point where he developed certain specifically female features (i.e., a sweet rack), which proves two things: First, if left unchecked, couvade syndrome can cause real problems. Second, if you want to show fabulous knockers on prime-time television, put them on a guy. I'm not saying it won't be profoundly disturbing, but at least you'll get to see them.

Okay, so you're not likely to go transgender, but you could certainly experience any number of bothersome sympathetic symptoms. Remember, I am not a doctor (I don't even play one on TV), so if you are experiencing real symptoms, don't hesitate to get them checked out. For less serious symptoms, here are a few things you could do to ease the pain.

Expose Them

Emotions get expressed one way or another. Either you face up to them and bring them out in the open, or they fester inside you and are expressed physically. If you notice yourself experiencing symptoms that are very similar to your wife's, tell your brain that you know what's going on, and you're not going to fall for it. I would recommend that you not do this out loud, especially not in public spaces with heavy security. If that doesn't work, you may need to take more drastic measures.

Try Actually Sympathizing

One reason you may be experiencing sympathy pain is because you're not doing any real sympathizing. Deep down inside, you may actually feel a little guilt and concern for what your wife is going through, and you have to pay your penance one way or another. I realize it's difficult, but try to be more supportive and caring with your wife when she's feeling particularly crappy (see "Head on Down to the Big Queasy"). You may find that the more you actually sympathize, the fewer sympathetic symptoms you'll have to endure.

Await the Cure

There is one surefire cure for sympathy pains: delivery. Once the baby is born, most likely all of your symptoms will disappear. Of course, they'll probably be replaced with stress headaches, back pain, and exhaustion. You may not end up feeling any better, but at least you'll know that the pain is all your own.

If you find that you do develop full-blown couvade syndrome and do develop sizeable "mammalian protuberances," you might as well make the best of them and do as Steve Martin suggested in *L.A. Story*: just sit around the house playing with your breasts all day.

HOW TO EMBRACE THE BABY SHOWER FOR FUN AND PROFIT

Difficulty 🍼🍼🍼   *Reward* 🍾🍾🍾🍾

Given the choice, most guys would probably prefer to attend a bachelorette party downtown at the Spicy Sausage rather than suffer through a baby shower. At least at a male strip club you might pick up a few good workout tips or dance moves. A baby shower offers nothing but a giggly gaggle of women oohing and aahing over ridiculously cute baby booties and other brightly colored infantalia. It's hardly an event at which any self-respecting man would be caught dead. It also may be an event where men are not wholly welcome. And if there's one thing no guy can abide, it's being denied admission to someplace he has no real desire to be. So, let's figure out the best way to inject yourself into the process, get what you want out of it, and have a grand old time along the way.

Man's aversion to the baby shower probably stems from the fact that the primary focus of the event is on girlie things like clothes, cute little toys, motherly indulgences, and nonerotic boob-related accessories. It's like a wedding shower without the risqué gag gifts (no pun intended). But it certainly doesn't have to be that way. Your goal is to expand the focus of the party to include items that are ostensibly for the baby but which, in fact, are really for you.

The best way to do this is to get involved in the baby provisioning process early on. As I mentioned before, pick a few items for which you'll be responsible, such as new technology (baby monitor, digital video camera, etc.) or hardware (crib, changing table, etc.). Then, when the baby shower starts to come together, make it clear that you've researched certain products and you want to make sure the brands you've chosen make it onto the gift registry. That way you can focus your energies on certain products, and not get overwhelmed thinking about all the other stuff, like clothing and diaper gear, that men can find so intimidating. Once you've infiltrated the system to this extent, you can begin transforming the entire event from within. And the possibilities are limitless.

First of all, you want to make sure the registry includes anything from your own childhood about which you feel particularly nostalgic. I used to love the book *Ferdinand the Bull* and my Cookie Monster doll. So once I had access to the registry, those were the first two things I added. And that was just the beginning. Once I got rolling, I ultimately was able to re-create my exact nursery room item for item, down to the Speed Racer crib sheets that I found on eBay.

Ultimately, your willing participation in the legitimate part of the baby shower gives you open license to bastardize the list to include any and all peripherally relevant items. The fact is that people love buying stuff for babies so much that they won't even notice that what they're buying is obviously for the baby's daddy. For example, I added the complete *Pee-Wee's Playhouse* series on DVD to our registry. Sounds like it's for kids, right? In fact, no child should ever watch that show, not because the material is inappropriate, but because the pace is so aggressively manic it could give a geriatric sloth ADHD. But at times it's absolutely brilliant, and it also features Laurence Fishburne as Cowboy

Curtis and the great Phil Hartman as Captain Carl. Here are a few other items you might want to sneak onto the registry:

Schoolhouse Rock!

You may remember these brilliant educational animated vignettes about grammar ("Conjunction Junction"), mathematics (the very groovy "3 Is a Magic Number"), and government ("I'm Just a Bill"). They originally aired in the 1970s and 1980s, and just about every kid at the time could recite all the lyrics. This special thirtieth-anniversary collection includes over fifty episodes, and while your kid probably won't appreciate it until he starts experimenting with drugs, you should take this opportunity to get it for yourself.

Creature Comforts

This collection of claymation shorts from the people who brought you the Wallace and Gromit movies is based on the hilarious Academy Award–winning short of the same name. Each piece includes a series of interviews with animals about their everyday lives. It's absolutely perfect for kids once they start watching television, but you'll enjoy it right now.

The Blue Planet

This astounding eight-part series from the BBC includes some of the most amazing footage you'll ever see of the Earth's oceans and its inhabitants. They're so good, I would recommend that you bump the *Baby Einstein* DVDs off your registry and add these. Plus, how could any child not be totally entranced by the melodically jittery voice of David Attenborough?

Just make sure you don't get greedy and start adding items that will reveal your scheme. For example, nobody will believe that a new Xbox, skybox tickets to Wrestlemania, and a complete build-it-yourself ice hockey rink are actually for the baby. And just in case you're thinking about it, The *Simpsons* and/or *South Park* DVDs definitely raise red flags.

HOW TO SATISFY HER EVERY CRAVING

Difficulty　　　　*Reward*

If only all of your wife's irrational impulses were as easy to satisfy as her pregnancy cravings. There's nothing subtle about a pregnancy craving, and she'll tell you in no uncertain terms exactly what she wants. If ever there were culinary aberrations for which men were perfectly suited to prepare, pregnancy cravings are just such freaks of food. In fact, the more bizarre the craving, the more it's likely to resemble an average male's typical late-night snack. So, rather than resist when she demands satisfaction, you should embrace her cravings and plan on making a little extra for yourself.

There's no clear consensus about what causes pregnancy cravings. Some studies have shown that women are likely to crave foods that satisfy certain dietary deficiencies—such as apples for calcium or potassium, olives for sodium, and peanut butter for protein and fat—but there are probably other factors at play as well. Some women crave comfort foods or foods from their childhood, which would indicate an emotional component. Cravings might also be tied to the change in a pregnant woman's sense of smell (see "Head on Down to the Big Queasy," above). Regardless of the causes, cravings are very real and usually undeniable.

In most cases, you'll just be dispatched to the supermarket to pick up a few half gallons of ice cream, a bag of chips, two tubes of chocolate chip cookie dough, and a can of lighter fluid (see "So Whatcha Want?" below). Don't question her on these, except to ask if there are any particular brands she wants. Regardless of her answer, be sure to buy a few different types of whatever foods she wants, since even the most subtle ingredient can spark a feeding frenzy or send her scampering to the can.

Don't think of this as an inconvenience, but rather as an opportunity. Remember, when you're out at the store you have carte blanche to pick up some of whatever you want for yourself, in the guise of anticipating her future cravings. So grab some Double Stuf Oreos and a big honkin' piece of meat while you're there. She'll think you're incredibly thoughtful, and you'll be all set when your own cravings hit.

For those instances where nothing store-bought will do the trick, I've got a few suggestions for you that are easy to prepare and that I know she'll love.

Salted Chocolate Balls

Say, everybody, have you seen my balls?
They're big and salty and brown.
—"SALTY CHOCOLATE BALLS," SUNG BY CHEF (*SOUTH PARK*)

I'm sure impregnation was the farthest thing from Chef's mind when he created his tantalizing treats, but this version is an all-in-one pregnancy cravings satisfier. A recent survey found that almost half of pregnant women craved sweets, while slightly fewer craved salty and sour foods (thus the infamous pickles and ice cream).

This dish, adapted from the fabulous Commerç 24 tapas bar in Barcelona, satisfies all three cravings. It's a truly weird dish that is ultimately completely decadent (in other words, perfect for the craving wife).

Makes about 12 balls.

8 ounces semisweet or bittersweet chocolate	3/4 cup heavy cream
1/4 cup olive oil	Salt*

Coarsely chop the chocolate, and place in a bowl. In a saucepan or in the microwave, heat the cream just until it comes to a boil. Pour the cream over the chocolate. Gently stir the mixture until the chocolate is melted and completely combined with the cream. Normally you'd let the chocolate cool at room temperature, but since your wife is probably getting impatient, you can put it in the fridge for about 45 minutes, or until firm. When it's chilled, scoop about a tablespoon of the chocolate at a time and roll it into balls. Drizzle olive oil over the top and sprinkle with salt.

Grilled Cheese with Just About Anything

My wife was heavily into nostalgia foods. We drove all over West L.A. in search of a malted milkshake that would do the trick (which, by the way, we found at Cafe 50's on Santa Monica Boulevard). Her most powerful craving by far was for grilled cheese sandwiches just the way she had them as a kid. We worked out the recipe until we got it just right, and then experimented with any

---

*The best salt to use for this is a flaky salt called Maldon, which you would need to get in advance at a specialty foods store. If you don't have it, use kosher salt.

number of variations. You can use any kind of cheese you like, but my wife found that the perfect cheese for her was the kind that Frank Zappa so aptly described as "that ugly, waxy fake yellow kind of cheese."

By the way, if your wife also has mostly nostalgic cravings, check out Todd Wilbur's *Top Secret Recipes* books, which include recipes for many classic snacks and candies.

Makes one sandwich, but you can multiply it ad infinitum (and ad nauseam).

2 slices of cheap white bread (Wonder works perfectly)
2 slices of processed cheese (or enough to make the wife happy)
1 tablespoon butter

Sandwich the cheese between the bread slices. Melt 1/2 tablespoon of the butter in a skillet, and grill the sandwich on one side until golden brown. Remove the sandwich, melt the other 1/2 tablespoon of butter, and grill on the other side.

Variations:

• Add hot sauce for a Mexican flair.
• Add pickles, potato chips, or just about anything else
  she's craving.
• Top the sandwich with chocolate sauce (I must admit that
  I came up with this one all on my own, and just the
  thought of it was enough to staunch my wife's cravings).

So Whatcha Want?

If you think craving grilled cheese sandwiches with chocolate sauce is weird (it's actually quite tasty, really), you'll be stunned by some of the things desired by women who experience a form of craving known as *pica*. From the Latin word for magpie (a bird that eats just about anything), pica refers to cravings for non-foods. Some common pica cravings include ice, hair, toothpaste, and even gasoline. As with "normal" cravings, there's no clear explanation for pica cravings, except possibly this: women are freaks. I don't yet have any hard data to back up this theory, but there is a wealth of anecdotal evidence.

HOW TO MAKE SURE YOU WIN THE NAME GAME

Difficulty *Reward*

Naming the baby may be the single toughest decision you and your wife need to make between conception and birth. It's a delicate negotiation, and one that men are poorly positioned to win. Because pregnancy has so little to do with guys, it's easy for us to disregard the significance of this decision, or deny how important it really is to us. Then, when we finally do jump into the debate, it's often just to agree to the one name that we're willing to accept, rather than helping to find one that we really like.

What's in a Name?

The gravity of the baby-naming decision is exacerbated by the assumption that the name you give a child will have a significant impact on that child's future. Expectant parents imagine their child's name being chanted at Fenway Park or Yankee Stadium. They wonder how it will sound with a Swedish accent at the Nobel ceremony, and they enunciate it slowly, including the middle initial, followed by "supergenius." The question is, does a name really matter? And, by extension, how much impact do parents have on their children's lives in general?

As it turns out, the answer to both questions is a resounding "not much." In their remarkable book *Freakonomics,* Steven Levitt and Stephen Dubner discuss Harvard economist Roland Fryer's analysis of birth certificate records to determine what impact a name has on that person's life. The data show that a name is important only in what it tells you about that person's background. The study clearly shows that certain types of parents tend to pick certain names for their children, and it's the socioeconomic status of the parents, not the kid's name per se, that can most accurately predict that child's future success or failure. So, what does this all mean to new parents?

Levitt and Dubner conclude, after exploring other parenting contexts, that besides the genes and the basic background we provide, all those countless conscious things we do as parents just don't have all that great an impact on who our kids become. So don't worry too much about which name you choose. By definition, if you choose it, it'll be the right name.

I believe that modern science will eventually discover that women have a gene for wanting to pick their baby's name, and that gene is switched on and immediately shifts into overdrive the second the woman becomes pregnant. It is essential that guys respond accordingly by expressing their philosophy on the subject of baby-naming. Rather than just summarily rejecting every name their wives suggest, guys need to tell their wives that they're just not ready to begin seriously thinking about what to name the baby. This is not because we are profoundly disinterested in the subject nine months before the baby will need his name. Quite the contrary: we want to take the time to let the fetus express itself, and for us to further understand how our lives as fathers will emerge. At least, that's the line I suggest you feed your wife.

In my case, I told my wife that I definitely wanted to hear the names she was thinking of, but I would only be ready to give the decision its due deliberation a few months before the due date. The advantage of this strategy is that my wife kept changing her mind (imagine that) about what kind of name she wanted. I just let her debate with herself, eliminating name after name without having to reveal any of my own opinions on the matter. Then, when the time came to get serious, I knew what her general preferences were, and I was able to refine my own list to fit within that framework and thus increase my chances of success. Another advantage of this strategy is that at some point your wife might actually suggest a name that you really like. In that case, don't let on that you like the name, but just tuck it away in the back of your mind. Eventually, you'll be able to whittle away all of her other suggestions and just be left with your favorite. The best way to do that is to develop a few strategies that will allow you to reject a ridiculous, horrible name without actually having to tell your wife that it's a ridiculous, horrible name.

1. Rejection by Association

If your wife is really enthusiastic about a name you just can't stand, one way to change her mind is to tell her that the name has a terribly negative association for you. Tell her that you knew someone in college by that name who could lift small change off the ground using only a strand of his own drool.

2. Rejection by Inappropriate Enthusiasm

This strategy is related to the previous one, but works on the opposite principle. Rather than tell her you can't accept the name, tell her you love it for a reason that she'll definitely hate. Let her know how cool you think it would be if your baby had the same name as the 2002 Professional Bull Riders world champion (it was Ednei Caminhas, in case you didn't know) or that talented stripper from your bachelor party. Here are a few examples of infamous people whose names you can drop to get your wife to drop her name:

- Sebastian: Lead singer for Skid Row (Sebastian Bach)
- Jake: Porn star who broke racial barrier (Jake Steed)
- Sarah: Like Sarah Connor from the *Terminator* movies. Repeat name in monotone Austrian accent until she relents.
- Olivia: Pig of children's literature (Olivia the Pig) or German drag queen (Olivia Jones)

3. Rejection by Insinuation

You can also use her maternal instincts against her when you want to reject a name. When she recommends a particularly wussy name, you can respond with, "That's a nice name, and I'm sure the relentless daily beatings he'll receive throughout grade school will ultimately build character."

Eventually, though, you're going to have to convince your wife that your favorite name is also the best one. Here are a few criteria you'll want to think about when making your case:

Try telling her that the name is a tribute to someone, such as a family member or important literary or historical figure, even if that's not who motivated you to select this name in the first place. In some cases, though, you may be better off not telling her the name's origin. For example, I have a friend from college, Eric Schmidt, who grew up near Philadelphia and was a huge Phillies fan as a kid. His wife, Tracy, knew nothing of baseball. Eric proposed that they name their first son Michael Jack (as in, Hall of Fame third baseman Michael Jack Schmidt), although he didn't share the source of his inspiration with her. They were just weeks away from the due date when a friend accidentally let Tracy in on the joke. She was not amused.

How Common Is the Name?
Is your wife the type to go along with the crowd (Emily, Jacob, Hannah), or will she prefer a more unique name (Dweezil, Apple, Phlebitis)?

What Does It Mean?
Google the name to see what comes up, and selectively use the citations that you know your wife will appreciate. In my case, after I came up with the name Azen (I just sort of made up the name and thought it sounded cool), I learned that the root *az* means *beloved* in Arabic. I didn't tell my wife until after he was born that an *azen* was a unit of measurement for tulip bulbs during the great Dutch tulip craze of the early 1600s.

How Does It Sound with the Last Name?

You definitely want to put your list of names up against the baby's last name and see how it sounds. This is another time when you'll want to consider your wife's sense of humor, and try to predict how she'll react to any novelty names. I'd suggest you avoid the patently absurd, like Providence, Rhode Island, mayor Buddy Cianci's (pronounced "see-AN-see") ex-wife Nancy Ann, or NASCAR driver Dick Trickle, and try to find a name that is both easy to say when coupled with the last name and doesn't suggest any urological maladies. I also recommend writing it down and seeing how it looks in print.

Does It Have Good or Bad Nickname Potential?

Some names just beg for adorable nicknames (a friend's baby Isabella goes by "Izzy" and we call our son "Azi"), while others can haunt a child forever (see Trickle, Dick).

Can You Picture the Kid at College with the Name?

This is a useful exercise when figuring out good names, but it also tugs at the wife's heartstrings and is likely to make her find the name appealing.

How Does It Compare?

When Martin Scorsese was shooting *Casino,* he included a particularly gruesome scene where Nicky Santoro (played by Joe Pesci, who else?) crushes a guy's head in a carpenter's vise. It was really just a throwaway scene, since Scorsese assumed the ratings board would instantly reject it as too violent. But he included it anyway, hoping it would make the film's other violent scenes seem tame by comparison. (As it turns out, the ratings board didn't reject the scene outright, but only recommended minor edits, like deleting the projectile eyeball.)

You can use this same strategy in convincing your wife to like your choice of names. Basically, tell her that you promised your great-uncle Ignatz on his deathbed that you'd name your first child after him. After all, he saved your life during a near-tragic badminton incident many years ago (or some such heroic deed). She will, of course, reject the name, but you should hold your ground. Eventually, though, you will concede to break your promise and not name your son Iggy or your daughter Ignatzia (regardless of the latter name's lyrical lilt). Then, when you tell your wife your next choice (your true favorite), it'll sound so good by comparison that she's bound to really like it.

Ultimately, though, when all is said and done, it's just a name. It won't seriously affect who your baby will become, although it could have a detrimental effect on you. Imagine if you put your foot down and insist on a name your wife doesn't like. Each and every time she utters that name it will resonate as a reminder that you are indebted to her forever. And even if you let her choose the name of all subsequent children, it will never compensate for your slight over naming the first. No name is worth relocating to that particular hell. And don't think that deferring to her earns you the right to any particular wifely largesse. In case you haven't yet noticed, marriage don't work that way, son.

HOW TO GET FIT FOR FATHERHOOD

Difficulty 🍼🍼🍼🍼 *Reward* 🍺🍺

Shortly after my son was born my wife and I watched the *Victoria's Secret Fashion Show* together (I Tivo'd it, if you must know). I watched intently, not just for the obvious reasons, but also to see if Heidi Klum could actually don those postage-stamp panties and the giant, fuzzy pink angel wings a scant few months after giving birth herself.

And there she was, apparently back to her double-digit fighting weight. She had survived nine months of pregnancy, the violation of physical laws that is childbirth, eight harrowing weeks of spit-up and sleep deprivation, and she was already back in shrineworthy shape and up there prowling the catwalk.

"That Heidi Klum really puts the 'gaunt' in gauntlet," I said to my wife, just then noticing that she, too, looked great. (Maybe not quite as great as Ms. Klum, but in all fairness my wife hadn't spent the past several weeks power-walking in stiletto heels with fifty-pound training wings strapped to her back.) She sat on the couch in a serene half-lotus—her back straight and tummy taught—and I realized that of the three of us, procreation had taken its most devastating toll on *me*. I had no excuse, what with my being a guy and all, and not actually having been pregnant.

If they could bounce back so quickly, then why couldn't I? After all, they'd actually carried their children to term, whereas my physical involvement in the process was over in mere minutes. They'd suffered through the hell of morning sickness, while

I could hardly summon even a perfunctory sympathy retch. They had given birth, while all I did during delivery was lend moral support and occasionally sneak out to relieve the birthing center fridge of several cookies-and-cream Luna bars. (The closest I'd ever come to giving birth was sophomore year in college, after eating the cook's infamous Dutch Dance-Off stew: one serving and you're clogged for days.)

And yet, there I sat, an exhausted, achy shell of my former self. These two women had gone through one of the most traumatic tests of endurance that the human body can suffer, and I was the one who felt like crap. How could that be?

Fatherhood had taken its toll on me, as it does so many other men. I had done a lifetime of bending, squatting, and lunging since the baby was born, and my shoulders, back, and knees were begging for mercy. Within two months I had a compressed disc and inflammation of a shoulder joint that required cortisone injections. Simply put, my little ten-pound butterball had completely kicked my ass.

Of course, no sane person would ever suggest that men have a harder time than women during the whole pregnancy and delivery process. But, as difficult a time as every woman has, at least they're somewhat prepared, and remarkably well designed to meet the challenges of pregnancy and delivery. Men, on the other hand, are totally uninformed and unprepared for the ordeal they'll face, and that makes the whole thing much harder than we would expect. Not that ignorance is an excuse, but it definitely explains why many men suffer disproportionately from the challenges they face.

As we'll see when we tackle the "New Father fifteen" below, there are many factors conspiring against men as they become fathers. First and most importantly, the physical challenges of fatherhood (including, but definitely not limited to the aforementioned bending, squatting, and lunging) target the areas of the body men are most likely to ignore, namely the neck, shoulders, and lower back. Second, since all of the emphasis on staying fit is directed toward the pregnant woman, men don't even realize that they're about to face a rather difficult physical challenge themselves.

As if becoming a father doesn't challenge your sense of masculinity enough, suddenly you'll find that the parts of the body that you've ignored all these years have become crucial to your daily routine. First, you may now have to pay attention to an area of your body known as the "pelvic girdle." No, it's not what they found Elvis wearing when he died. It refers to the skeletal structure of your upper hips, which supports your torso and connects it to your legs.

Next, you'll need to concentrate on your "core." Up until now you probably just snickered derisively whenever you'd hear the ladies talk about the importance of strengthening their cores, figuring it was probably something they'd picked up on Oprah. In fact, the core refers to the band of muscles circling your abdomen around to your spine and also includes your butt, hips, and upper thighs. With a new baby around, this area will be challenged like never before. Unfortunately, no amount of bench presses or curls will help you if you're weak in the core, so we're going to have to change things a bit from your normal workout.

Try Pilates

Strengthening the core is one of the central themes of the Pilates exercise regimen. Once again, you may think we're in exclusively feminine territory, but Joseph Pilates created his method for men

Would you tell Joseph Pilates that his workout is just for girls?

and women alike, and it's a serious workout. More importantly, it focuses directly on your most underdeveloped muscles, and those that will become most important to you in the coming months.

I definitely recommend taking a Pilates class during your wife's pregnancy (maybe take classes with her, as after the baby arrives you'll have a tough time doing anything together outside the house). But even if you don't start a class, you really should begin doing some exercises to help with your core strength and flexibility.

The most important reason to increase your core strength and flexibility is because once the baby arrives, it becomes virtually impossible to rest any injury sufficiently for a full recovery. In my case, my shoulder started hurting only a week or so after the baby was born, when I was carrying him in a sling on a hike (bad idea, I know). It got worse and worse, such that every time I picked up the baby I was in serious pain. Virtually everything I did engaged the inflamed joint. After medication, physical therapy, and injections, I was still experiencing pain, albeit much less severely, a full year after the initial onset.

Pilates will help with your flexibility and strength in ways that will directly benefit you as a new father. Of course, be sure to talk to your doctor if you think you may have any problems with these exercises, and always stop if you feel any pain (beyond what you would expect from the stretches).

Posture

Besides strengthening your core with Pilates, improving posture is probably the easiest way to protect against injury. Especially for men who work at computers much of the day, there's a tendency to hunch over and roll your shoulders forward. If you work out your chest more than your back, as most men do, you're just reinforcing bad posture. Whenever you think about it, remind yourself to bring your shoulder blades back and down, as if you were trying to stick them in your back pocket. This is especially important when you're bending over to pick up the baby. You always want to keep your back straight, bend with your knees, keep your shoulders back and down, and stick your butt out. It's not terribly graceful, I know, but neither is sprawling out flat on your back, sobbing. The more you practice it, the easier it will become, the more it will help, and the less you'll care how ridiculous you look. Here's one way to test if you're bending incorrectly: if every time you bend over to pick up the kid something falls from your breast pocket and bonks him on the head, you need to straighten your back.

Of course, sometimes you just can't bend with your knees.

For example, when you're taking the baby from his car seat, you need to bend at the waist to get in there. This is a particularly dangerous move, since it really puts a lot of extra strain on your shoulders and lower back. When you absolutely must bend over at the waist, one thing you can do to help prevent injury is to "engage" or "brace" your abs. This is another core element of Pilates, and it involves pulling your abs in as tight as you can. You can think of it as if there's a string between your belly button and your spine, and you want to pull that string so that your belly comes in as close to your spine as possible. Any time you need to bend or lift in an awkward position, engage your abs to help protect against injury.

Stretching

Stretching is another necessary activity that most men ignore. Deep down inside, we all believe we're still that spry eighteen-year-old who can jump right into the game and recover from any injury overnight. Unfortunately, we often learn the painful truth (literally) after it's too late. The simple fact is that stretching is beneficial at any age, but it becomes much more so the older we get.

The Stretches

Hold each stretch for ten breaths. Repeat three times each.

1. HAMSTRING STRETCH

If you do no other stretching at all, do this one. Tight hamstrings can contribute to the joyful condition known as sciatica, which is experienced by shooting pains down the back of the legs. If you think the baby could keep you up at night, he's got nothing on sciatica.

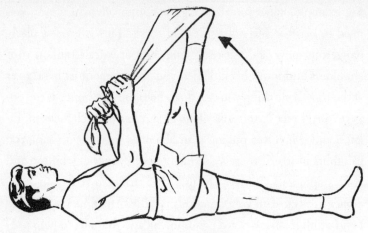

Hamstring Stretch

- Lie on your back and press your lower back to the ground.
- Loop a strap or a belt around 1 foot, and raise that leg straight up.
- When you feel the stretch, hold it for ten breaths. Switch legs and repeat three times.
- Variation: After you bring the leg up, pull it across your body until you feel the stretch further along the outside of your thigh.

2. HIP AND BUTT STRETCH

These stretches are also crucial for keeping the muscles deep in your hip and your glutes loose, which helps alleviate the stress placed on your lower back.

- Get into pushup position, keeping your pelvis straight.
- Bring your left knee forward, pointing your left foot across your body to the right.

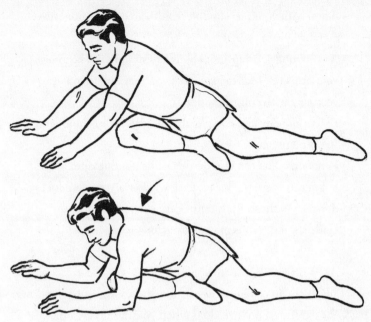

Hip and Butt Stretch

- Point your right foot back behind you.
- Lean forward down onto your forearms, and bring your upper body down toward the ground.
- You should feel the stretch deep inside your left hip. You can twist your body a bit in either direction to adjust the location of the stretch.
- Hold for ten breaths and then switch legs. Repeat three times.

3. SHOULDER SHRUGS

We all hold lots of tension in our shoulders and necks, and this is a great stretch to loosen up those areas and relieve that tension.

- Stand with your feet shoulder-width apart and your arms comfortably at your side.
- As you inhale, bring your shoulders straight up, keeping your arms relaxed. Imagine that you're trying to touch your ears with your shoulder.
- Exhale quickly and completely, and drop your shoulders. Repeat ten times.
- Variations: You can also do this while holding dumbbells, but in this case you'll want to slowly lower your shoulders down from the top position. Also, you may want to include shoulder rolls in your stretching regimen.

4. LOWER BACK PRESS

This is an excellent exercise for stretching out your lower back. Be careful to not overdo it when you're starting out.

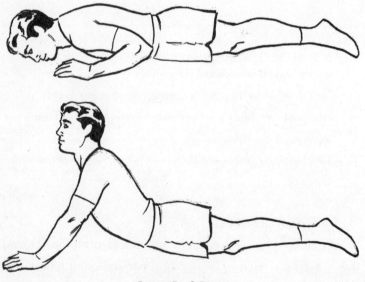

Lower Back Press

- Lie on your stomach with your feet pointing behind you, keeping your elbows tucked in and your hands on the ground above your shoulders.
- Look straight ahead and keep your lower back and buttocks relaxed.
- As you inhale, slowly raise yourself up on your forearms as high as possible, keeping your hips on the floor. For a deeper stretch, you can extend your arms and raise your upper body up further.
- Keep breathing, and hold the stretch for three deep breaths.

Strengthening

I've decided to consider it a good thing that the strengthening exercises we'll focus on have little or nothing to do with how jacked you'll appear poolside. Those exercises—curls, bench presses, military presses, and so on—just won't help where you really need it. If you can summon the energy to keep doing them, go for it, but with a baby around the only thing you're likely to press is the snooze button in a vain attempt to get a few extra minutes of sleep. Besides, you're married with a kid now. Who are you trying to impress? This is one time in your life when it's definitely more important to feel good than to look good, and to do that you need to start at the core.

For these exercises, I would suggest doing two sets of ten or twenty repetitions, depending on your level of fitness. Eventually try to get up to thirty reps.

1. SIT-UP

Guess what? Your least favorite strengthening exercise is probably the most important for preventing back pain. That's right, the sit-up, or in this case a slight alteration on the classic sit-up.

Strengthening your abs is crucial for maintaining good upper-body stability and taking pressure off your back. And while you'll probably never get six-pack abs, doing this exercise can help trim a few inches off the gut.

- Lie on your back and fold your arms across your chest.
- Engage your abs, flattening your lower back down to the floor.
- Exhale as you raise your shoulders up off the floor, focusing on tightening your abs even further.
- Hold at the top for a moment, then slowly lower your shoulders down to the ground as you inhale.

2. BRIDGE

Since you're already on the floor doing your sit-ups, why not do another exercise that is great for core stabilization, as well as your upper quads?

- Lie on your back with your arms at your side.
- Engage your abs, flattening your lower back down to the floor.

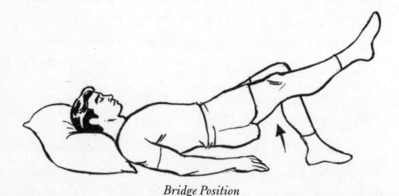

Bridge Position

- Lift your butt up so that there's just a slight angle between your thigh and your belly.
- Extend one leg up until your thighs are parallel to each other.
- Hold this for three breaths, and then lower your leg back to the starting position.
- Repeat the exercise three times on both sides.

3. MIDBACK/SHOULDER BLADE STABILIZATION

Another important area that most men neglect is the midback, from the bottom of your shoulder blades down to your lower back. I know that in my case about half of my back pain hits this area, such that I feel as if I've got a knife stuck under one shoulder blade (see "Oy, Your Aching Back," below). These exercises will help protect against that pain, and will also provide important stabilization for the lower back as well.

- Lie on your stomach with your arms straight out to your sides and your hands facing forward.

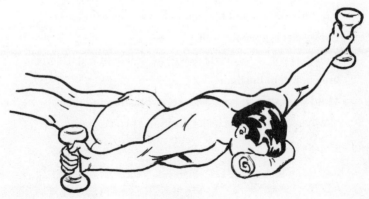

Shoulder Press

- Exhale as you bring your shoulder blades together, lifting your arms off the floor.
- Hold for three breaths, and then slowly release your shoulder blades and lower your arms as you inhale.
- Variations: You can use small dumbbells with this exercise, or anything you have handy around the house (cans of soup work well). You can also try this exercise with your arms straight up above your head, or straight back along your body. In both cases your palms should be turned inward.

4. WALL SQUAT

Many guys will find this exercise very easy, but it's definitely good to do. You can always hold the position longer to challenge yourself. Not only will this work your quads and strengthen your core, it's good practice for bending with your knees while keeping your back straight.

- Stand with your back against a wall and put your heels about a foot or so from the wall.
- Engage your abs and tilt your pelvis so that your lower back is flat against the wall.
- Inhale as you slowly slide down the wall until your thighs are parallel to the floor.
- Hold this position for at least three breaths, and then slowly return to the starting position as you exhale.

Am I Not a Man?

As I mentioned before, getting fit for fatherhood isn't about working out your chest and arms. Basically, since almost every guy overemphasizes these muscles, I wanted to make sure I got to everything else first. Now we can take a moment to talk about the old classics. I wouldn't suggest that you not do any chest or arm work, but try to stay balanced. Make sure you work out your shoulders and back as much as you do your chest and arms. I might even suggest that you do slightly less work on your chest and arms, since those muscles will be getting constant work as you lift the baby, crawl around, and get into all of the various monkey-like gyrations involved in fatherhood.

OY, YOUR ACHING BACK

How to Avoid the Backache Burden

Difficulty   *Reward*

If you've never been whacked in the sacrum with a pool cue or had a shiv stuck between your shoulder blades, you're in for a real treat. Fatherhood readily provides many such memorable sensations. Even under normal circumstances, men are likely to suffer from back pain at some point. When you add in all the new and potentially debilitating activities of fatherhood—squatting, sitting cross-legged, and general baby-hauling—it's hard to imagine any new father escaping the scourge.

Besides getting in better shape and increasing your flexibility, there are a couple of other strategies that might help alleviate your suffering:

1. DRINK PLENTY OF WATER

There are lots of studies showing that dehydration can play a significant role in back pain. The lower back muscles are more likely to go into spasm when dehydrated, and new fathers are definitely prone to dehydration. I know that when I worked in an office, gathering around the water cooler wasn't just a cliché. Regardless of the motivation (which was usually just procrastination), I spent plenty of time in the office kitchen, and drank plenty of water. When I was at home, particularly after the baby arrived, I realized that I would go for hours without drinking any water. On top of that, not only do caffeinated and alcoholic drinks not count toward your daily fluid intake, they actually count against the total (damn those eggheads at the FDA!) since they result in a net loss of water in the body. Here are some tips to help you get enough water every day:

- It is recommended that you drink about half your weight in ounces of water every day. So if you weigh 180 pounds, you should drink about 90 ounces of water every day.

- Don't wait until you're thirsty to start drinking. You should be drinking small amounts constantly throughout the day, rather than waiting until you're parched and chugging a bucketful.

- Keep a water bottle with you at all times. A new baby can and will throw your life into complete chaos at any time, so having a bottle at hand makes it much more likely that you'll drink regularly.

- As I mentioned above, caffeine and alcohol are diuretics and decrease the water in the body. So if you drink coffee or partake of a much-needed midnap martini, you should add the same amount of extra water to your daily total. Also, since you're maintaining some workout schedule (I hope), you should add a glass of water for every twenty minutes of active exercise.

2. RELEASE YOUR RAGE

There's a school of thought that says back pain is psychosomatic, which basically means that it's caused by some mental stress rather than a physical trauma. That doesn't mean there isn't a real muscle or nerve injury, or that the pain isn't real. It just means that the initial instigator of the injury is mental (just like the way an ulcer can be stress-induced). The leading proponent of this theory is Dr. John E. Sarno, author of *Healing Back Pain: The Mind-Body Connection.* You may have heard Dr. Sarno being touted by Howard Stern, who credits Sarno with curing his chronic back pain.

Sarno's core theory is that the brain uses the back as a way to express stress and rage that we can't admit to ourselves consciously. And fatherhood is full of such stressors. Here's how Sarno's theory would apply to new fathers:

1. The new father is under great stress. He's often completely frustrated. He feels lots of pressure to be the perfect dad

and be completely happy and completely in love with the new baby. He isn't any of those things.

2. The mind won't let him acknowledge these feelings consciously, and looks for another way to express them.

3. Since his back is also under great strain as a new parent, his brain decides that that would be a perfect place to express those feelings physically, and he'll just assume that the pain is due to the squatting and lifting, rather than the guilt and the rage.

I realize that it all seems a bit too weird, but if anyone would experience this type of phenomenon, it's a new dad, and Sarno does have a very respectable success rate with his patients.

So, how do you get rid of the pain? First of all, you have to express those feelings of frustration, anger, and guilt that are perfectly normal for new dads. That's why I tell every expectant father I meet that the first few weeks of fatherhood totally suck (see "How to Accept That the First Few Weeks Totally Suck"), and that guys are poorly equipped to handle it, both mentally and physically. If you can admit that to yourself, it'll go a long way toward alleviating the stress, frustration, and, I hope, the back pain that often accompany new fatherhood.

HOW TO AVOID THE NEW FATHER FIFTEEN

Difficulty 🍼🍼🍼🍼   *Reward* 🍺🍺

I did absolutely no physical preparation for fatherhood, and as I mentioned, shortly after the baby was born I developed severe pain in my shoulder and lower back. I went to see the doctor, and before my appointment I weighed in with the nurse. Ever since college I have been somewhere between 175 and 180 pounds, so you can imagine my shock when the nurse belted out plainly for all to hear, "One ninety-seven! You're pushing two bills there, kiddo." "That can't be right," I said, "I've never been close to that weight before." "Oh, it's right," she shot back.

I had fallen victim to a completely overlooked scourge of new fatherhood, the New Father Fifteen. Always being an overachiever, I actually accomplished a New Father Nineteen. How could this have happened? Actually, after giving it a moment's thought, it's amazing that I didn't see it happening. Becoming a father presents the perfect storm of factors for packing on the pounds: increased food intake, less physical activity, and greater stress.

First, there's the increased food intake. This is mostly your wife's fault, since she was increasing her food intake throughout her pregnancy, and it's hard not to follow her lead. Of course, she's got an excuse for doing so (i.e., she's growing another human being inside her body). You're just bingeing by association.

Next, in all likelihood the amount of exercise you do will drop off precipitously after the baby arrives, if not before. This, coupled with increased food intake, presents a big problem for men. As I mentioned earlier, there is probably a significant testosterone drop after the baby is born. This translates into a loss of lean muscle mass, which in turn can slow your metabolism. That means that at the same time as you're eating more and exercising less, your metabolism downshifts, resulting in the potential for significant weight gain.

And all the stress doesn't help. I don't believe that becoming a father is the most stressful event of your life (I found buying a house much worse), but it creates a heightened level of stress over a very long period of time, and that takes its toll. Plus, stress is a likely cause of couvade syndrome, which causes some men to experience the same symptoms of pregnancy as their wives (see "How to Avoid Sympathy Pains," above). The weight gain could be a result of, don't laugh, relating *too much* with your wife. Hey, there's a first time for everything.

On top of all those factors, there's a general tendency of men to ignore what's going on with our bodies. We're just no good at it, especially compared with women, going way back to when we were kids. As girls approach puberty, they confront the changes to their bodies openly, and their mothers usually lead them through it. For boys, puberty is a bewildering, embarrassing experience, and their dads are usually no help at all. By the time they're fathers themselves, they've been fully indoctrinated in the male inclination to suppress or ignore all but the most extreme physical and mental difficulties, often with potentially serious consequences. For example, some men actually experience brief sexual arousal when playing with their babies. Researchers consider this normal, and theorize that it's the result of men improperly compartmentalizing emotional and physical responses to stimuli. So if this happens to you, don't go running out to the castration clinic just yet. You're probably not a pedophile; you're just a "normal" guy (as scary a thought as that may be).

Further compounding our cluelessness is the fact that all of the emphasis on health and diet is directed toward your wife and what she needs to do before, during, and after pregnancy. Virtually every pregnant woman has a plan in mind for how she's going to get her body back after delivery. And societal pressures make sure she sticks with it. Oh, if only we were lucky enough to have the constant motivation provided by a smothering societal emphasis on unattainable bodily perfection the way women do. To be honest, men also tend to concentrate exclusively on their wives' plans, further adding to the pressure on women, and give no thought to creating or executing their own plans. Well, the time has come to do just that.

Eat Less (and Better)

Early fatherhood is no time to radically overhaul your eating habits. You've got way too much going on, and the last thing you want is a diet adding any extra stress to your life. Nonetheless, this is a particularly bad time to be eating poorly, so here are just a few simple suggestions that can help you keep your weight down:

1. GET WET

It's really easy for new fathers to drink too little water. Increasing your water intake, besides helping prevent muscle pain, can also help curb your appetite.

2. GO NUTS

Almonds are probably the single best snack you can have. They provide lots of protein for building muscle, and they contain the monounsaturated fats that can boost your testosterone to help with muscle growth and fat-burning. Plus they fill you up fast and keep you feeling full longer. It's best to eat almonds with the skins on. You can also try peanut butter, but if you're going to eat it by the spoonful, go with unsalted. By the way, olive oil is another excellent source of monounsaturated fats.

3. BREAK AN EGG

Eggs have gotten a bad rap over the years, but research is now revealing their true benefits. These include very efficient protein for building muscle, and lots of vitamin B_{12} to help break down fat.

4. STAY WHOLE

You've got to have carbs in your diet, so make sure you're eating the right ones. The whole grains in brown rice and whole wheat products help keep your insulin levels low, which prevents the body from storing fat.

5. GET MOVING

Certain exercises are great for suppressing your appetite. The key is keeping your temperature high. That's why running curbs your appetite while swimming makes you hungry. It's also possible that the intensity level of your workout also affects appetite, with some studies showing that more intense workouts curb hunger longer.

If you want to learn more about optimum nutrition, as well as great exercise suggestions for new dads, there's an excellent book called *The Abs Diet* by David Zinczenko, the editor-in-chief of *Men's Health*, and Ted Spiker.

Exercise More

As we just saw, intense exercise that elevates your body temperature is best for curbing your appetite. But since it's often very difficult to get to the gym with a new baby in the house, you need to give some serious thought to how you're going to stay as active as possible.

1. GET ON SCHEDULE

I'm a big proponent of getting your baby on a set schedule as soon as possible. I believe that this is good for the baby, but equally important, I know it's good for dads (see "How to Maintain the Illusion of Control" in the next chapter). The sooner your baby has a set routine, the sooner you will, and with luck that can include time for exercise.

2. GO OUT OF YOUR WAY

Lots of parenting books will suggest ways to make your life more efficient around the house. For example, some will suggest that you set up changing stations in a few different places so you won't have to go far when the baby needs changing. I'd suggest you only have one place to change the baby, so that at least you'll get that little extra walk, possibly upstairs, when it's time for a change. Look around for other ways to keep moving around the house. Every little bit helps.

3. GET WALKING

Many guys disregard walking as not being strenuous enough. But face it, you're getting older, and your time is more limited, and

Carrying the baby does present certain risks.

walking with the baby is a great way to bond and get a little exercise without stressing your knees and back too much. And walking with the baby doesn't have to be so easy. Carrying the baby in a Bjorn or a backpack can transform a walk or a hike into a serious workout. Keep in mind that when the baby gets to a certain size, the Bjorn can become dangerous, exposing your windpipe to a backward head butt and your crotch to an agonizing dolphin kick.

If you can find the time, definitely try to do more strenuous cardiovascular exercise that gets your heart rate going to about 50 to 75 percent of your maximum heart rate, which is roughly calculated as 220 minus your age. For example, if you're thirty years old, your maximum heart rate is 220−30, or 190 beats per minute. The range you're shooting for is 50 to 75 percent of 190, or 95 to 142 bpm.

You should really strive to get some form of exercise for at least thirty minutes most days. Not only will you burn calories, but you'll also increase the length of time you can hold your breath, which will come in handy during those particularly nasty diaper changes (see "How to Change Diapers: The Taming of the Poo").

Reduce Stress

Regular exercise is particularly important for new fathers, since it's a great way to reduce stress. Another strategy is to start meditating (see "How to Become a Zen Master Daddy"). Meditation doesn't need to be a complex spiritual regimen; it only needs to be quiet time on your own when you can clear your mind. With a new baby in the house, quiet time alone becomes a precious commodity indeed.

All that being said, you will get some help along the way. For example, each time the baby gets the runs, you'll probably lose your appetite for a day or so. Once he starts walking, you'll get plenty of exercise. And it's hard to be stressed out when you're unconscious from exhaustion.

I don't know about you, but I feel better just talking about it. It may just be the testosterone deficiency, but it sure seems clear to me that women are on to something when they confront their feelings and their behaviors head-on. I'll admit it. I'm not afraid to expose my feminine side. As long as I never have to be pregnant, how bad can it be?

WHOA. BABY!

Ready or Not, You Are Now a Dad

Among the many futile obsessions occupying twenty-first-century men is our relentless pursuit of control. We're forever striving to control our environment, our wives, and ourselves, with consistently abysmal results. And of the universe of events that we might attempt to control, the single most uncontrollable is the birth of our child. The best we can hope for is to get through the whole ordeal with something resembling dignity. Short of that, we'd at least like to have a funny story to tell the kid when he's old enough to appreciate it. For example:

A month before my son was due, I was blissfully sleeping the sleep of the clueless. I dreamt that my wife gave birth to a well-spoken, potty-trained toddler, like Stewie from *Family Guy,* minus the sadism. Around 2:00 A.M. I was jostled awake by my wife, who said with quickly evaporating placidity, "I think my water broke." I muttered something incomprehensible into the darkness. "Seriously," she said. "I'm pretty sure my water just broke." We had only made it halfway through our birthing class, but instinctively I knew just what to do and I sprang into action. "Yeah, right," I said, and promptly went back to sleep. After that, all I remember is a glancing blow to the head (I think it was a shampoo bottle, or maybe an ironing board), and the next thing I knew I was behind the wheel driving to the hospital. Twenty-seven hours later I was a daddy.

That's how it happens, agonizingly protracted yet ultimately instantaneous, and afterward you can't distinguish day from night or up from down. But that's all for the best, since the last thing you'll want when you hold your child in your arms for the first time is a lucid sense of reality. Although, for the foreseeable future, that hazy, disorienting dizziness *is* your reality, so you might as well get used to it.

HOW TO REMAIN CONSCIOUS DURING DELIVERY

Difficulty   *Reward (no kidding)*

On the one hand, you might find it comforting to know that almost every guy worries that he might pass out or throw up during delivery. On the other hand, that fact alone is evidence enough that most men are ridiculously ill prepared for parenthood, which is discomforting. On the third hand, knowing that we're all incompetent and seeing that most of us manage to get through it just fine anyway is comforting. On yet another hand, not knowing how all those other guys did it is discomforting.

I was definitely one of those guys who worried that he'd pass out during delivery. In fact, I couldn't possibly imagine a scenario in which I wouldn't end up kissing linoleum. Every time I'd see pictures of friends in the hospital with their newborn babies, I'd always scan their eyes for some hint of what they had just seen, or some indication as to how I could get through it myself without making a complete ass of myself. When I'd ask the new dads about it, they'd always say something like, "It was amazing. I was totally relaxed and just focused on what I had to do to help my wife." I tried to believe them, but I just couldn't imagine that I would ever describe my experience in those terms, or even remember the experience at all.

Well, I've now been through it myself, and let me just tell you that it was amazing. I was totally relaxed and just focused on what I had to do to help my wife. I know it's hard to believe, but someday you will describe the experience in those terms as well. Besides just trusting me on this, which I can't recommend with a straight face, here are some other things you can do to prepare yourself.

First of all, ignorance is your worst enemy here. You definitely want to take a birthing class that will walk you through the entire process. The more you know, the less terrifying it all becomes. One thing that you'll very quickly come to realize is that almost every representation of childbirth you've seen on television is wildly unrealistic. For one thing, you don't see the hours and hours of inactivity that generally precede active labor. In reality, when it's actually time for delivery, you're so excited to have something to do you'll forget how traumatic it should be.

Plus, you need to be aware that a newborn baby does not look like the smiley, cherubic little angel that you see on TV. So-called newborns on TV are actually several months old. As sick as the culture of stage mothers is in this country, it's not so sick as to drive a mother to bring her actual newborn to a screen test. I've decided to find that reassuring. In fact, newborn babies are quite hideous, all blotchy and slimy, with oblong heads and swollen genitalia. It's not surprising, given what they've just been through, but it can be somewhat startling nonetheless.

Next, you'll want to have as complete a sense as possible of how to support your wife during labor and delivery. Granted, neither of you know exactly what to expect, but you should discuss generally how you want to work together. For example, my wife approached delivery much like an athletic event, so she wanted me to be like a spotter in the gym or a trainer on the track, urging her on and helping her stay focused. You've already gotten a lot of practice helping her with morning sickness, cravings, and other oddities of pregnancy, so delivery is really just an extension of those.

Another way to stay focused (and vertical) is to be the master of the birthing plan. This is a crucial role, not only because you need to make sure your wife gets everything she needs and all of your questions get answered, but also because it'll give you a much-needed (if illusory) sense of control. Be forewarned, though, that if your plan includes the possibility of an epidural, do not look at the needle, which is so large that you'll likely experience a touch of penis envy just before everything goes black.

Finally, you definitely want to take care of yourself during what can be quite a lengthy ordeal. Get some sleep when you can, be sure to eat well, and drink plenty of fluids. Try to get outside for some fresh air and maybe even a little exercise. You also don't want to incur any painful injuries during delivery. One such injury can result from an improper grip when you're holding your wife's hand. If she grabs your hand around the fingers, a sudden contraction could cause her to grip so hard that she does real damage. Instead, use a "soul brother" grip where you interlock your thumbs. That way, when she grips tight she'll just be squeezing the fleshy part around your thumb.

Most importantly, you should know that you're going to be fine. The anticipation is much more traumatic than the event itself. When you're there in the delivery room, you'll be so keyed up focusing on your wife and helping her that the baby's arrival may actually be anticlimactic. It may be hours or even days before things settle down enough to appreciate what has happened, and you think to yourself, *Holy shit! I'm a dad.* Now *that's* when you're likely to pass out.

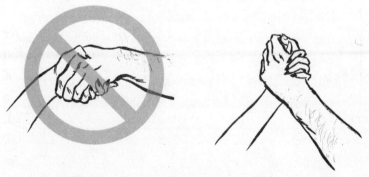

The proper way to hold hands during delivery.

A Thief in the Night

Ah, the mother lode.

—KRAMER (MICHAEL RICHARDS), ON *SEINFELD*, UPON
DISCOVERING THE HOSPITAL'S STASH OF RUBBER GLOVES

There are few creatures more inclined to petty thievery than an alternately anxious and bored father-to-be cut loose in a dark, deserted maternity ward in the wee small hours. Before I continue, maybe I should have the suits over in legal look into the statute of limitations on linen theft. Assuming I'm in the clear, allow me to give you a few tips to help pass the time and stock the nursery.

First of all, you can never have too many washcloths. For the next several months your baby will be leaking from every conceivable orifice (our son had earned himself the nickname "SpongeBib SparePants"), and you'll need to have something on hand to wipe him with. Actually, I recommend that you buy one of those retractable keychains and fasten a washcloth to it. That way, you'll always have a Handi Wipe right on your hip.

Beyond the washcloths, onesies, and other assorted linens, most hospital supply closets are stocked with things you may have no obvious use for, but that nonetheless look really appealing. While I can't condone stealing for no reason other than that you've got nothing better to do, I can recommend a good excuse to use if you get caught. Simply let the tears well up, and with your voice trembling, say, "My baby needs a gross of powder-free, nonlatex rubber gloves, dammit. I only did it for my baby!!" Congratulations, you've just discovered the joys of using your baby to get away with stuff (see "How to Use the Baby to Get Away with Just About Anything").

HOW TO ACCEPT THAT THE FIRST FEW WEEKS TOTALLY SUCK

Difficulty 🍼🍼🍼   *Reward* 🍺

I was riding in an elevator in New York awhile back with a new father and his tiny newborn baby. "How old?" I asked. "Two weeks," he answered wearily. "I've got a ten-month-old," I said. He looked up from the stroller and asked—pleadingly and with more emotional yearning than I've ever seen in any guy east of Brokeback Mountain—"It gets better, right?" "Yeah, definitely," I said sincerely. He seemed genuinely relieved.

To be perfectly honest, the first few weeks of fatherhood just suck. That's right, you heard me. They're awful. I said it, and I'm not taking it back (I will, though, drop a C-note in the Therapy Jar). Everyone tells you how blessed you are and how thrilled you must be, and you keep asking yourself, "What have these people been smoking?"

You may be thinking, "Why would you tell me this? I'm already freaking out about the whole fatherhood thing, and now you tell me it sucks!?! What gives?" Bear with me, guys, because it all works out in the end. And besides, knowing what's coming can making the whole thing easier (and guilt-free).

Here's the scenario: The adrenalin rush of delivery is receding, all the well-wishers have come and gone, and you're slowly beginning to realize that you're in it, and there's no getting out. You and your wife struggle to figure out how to manage caring for this little creature 24/7, and sometimes it feels like it's literally 24/7. You're exhausted, stressed, and totally unsure about almost everything you're doing. But it's all worth it, because you feel a more profound love for your child than you ever imagined, right? Wrong! In all likelihood, you feel little or no real connection or bond with the baby. You're busting your butt for this kid, and you're getting nothing in return except more dirty diapers, spit-up, and sleepless nights. Your friends tell you it will get better, but this nagging thought keeps popping into your head: could it be that parenting is, at best, just another form of Stockholm syndrome*?

You feel awful and guilty just thinking about it. What kind of father doesn't love his newborn baby? You start asking yourself if you'll ever love this baby, and you imagine year after year of indifferent servitude stretching into the distant future. Like I said, it sucks. But admitting that it sucks really helps. I hope that by being completely honest with you, you might avoid that guilt and feel more confident than I did that the love and the bond will come soon enough. After about five weeks or so, the baby flashes his first smile, and your heart melts. You've made it through that tough initial adjustment, and it really does get better and better.

If you learn anything from those first few weeks, it's that it's best to be honest with yourself. If you screw up (make that "*when* you screw up"), lose your temper, or wish you had your old life back, don't be too hard on yourself afterward. Mistakes and feelings of ambivalence don't make you a failure; they make you normal. We've all had those feelings at some point, and we

---

*Stockholm syndrome is a phenomenon whereby hostages (new parents, in this case) develop sympathy for and loyalty to their captor (the baby). The name comes from a 1973 bank robbery in Stockholm in which the hostages appeared to bond with the robbers during their captivity, and even defended them afterward.

turned out fine. And unless your address is Neverland Ranch, California, you'll do just fine, too.

Build the Team

Those first few weeks should be like spring training for you and your wife. It's time to start working together as a team to make caring for the baby as efficient a process as possible. I'm not saying you should split the work evenly, but you need to figure out what each of your roles should be and how best to fulfill them. For example, if you're making the money for the family at a stressful job, she needs to cut you some slack and let you have some down time (don't think you won't be working your ass off around the house with a new baby, but you should be able to do it less than guys with easier and more flexible jobs).

The most important thing to remember is that you share a common goal, and that you're working together to get there. Every once in a while you'll want to offer a little extra help, since your wife is really bearing the brunt of the parenting during this time. I guarantee that she'll appreciate the offer, but you must make sure that you actually follow through. Otherwise, you stand to make things much worse. For example, one friend of mine decided that he would take over the nighttime feedings for a night so that his wife could finally get a full night's sleep. The next morning he woke up all excited. He nudged his wife awake and gleefully proclaimed, "She did it! The baby slept through the night!" "Not exactly," his wife mumbled drowsily. "She was up three times. *You* slept through the night." The moral of this story is: an offer unfulfilled is worse than no offer at all.

When you do offer extra help and successfully follow through, don't think that earns you a pass next time there's extra work to be done. It's kind of like the situation with the national debt. We run up this huge debt over decades, and as soon as we're fortunate enough to actually have a little bit of a surplus and can cut into that debt, we congratulate ourselves with a big tax cut and the debt goes even higher. I can guarantee that you owe your wife a debt as far as parenting goes. So when you finally go above and beyond, don't think that you've earned a vacation. Just keep quiet and consider yourself lucky.

Getting in Touch

A mother and her newborn obviously share a powerful physical bond, which in many cases is reinforced immediately after birth through breastfeeding. Many new fathers find it frustrating that they're not afforded the same connection. If you want to feel some form of tactile connection while feeding your baby, there is something you can do. My son was born a month early and was unable to breast-feed right away, so a lactation consultant suggested we feed him pumped breast milk through a periodontal syringe.

It is a very simple procedure: I would fill the syringe with milk, then put the little finger of my other hand in the baby's mouth and press it gently against his upper palette to trigger the sucking reflex. I would then position the tip of the syringe next to my fingertip and slowly deliver the milk as the baby sucked.

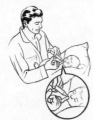

Feeding the baby this way was a really cool experience. Even if you don't need to use this technique, I would suggest that you ask your pediatrician if you can do it anyway every once in a while.

New fathers can participate in early feedings.

Face Your Fears

Up until now, fatherhood has been an abstract concept. You could imagine yourself in the role and you'd either feel confident, hesitant, or terrified. That abstraction is now reality, and you've got to deal with it. Luckily, when you've got no choice but to adapt, you usually do, and in this case you'll probably find that nothing is as bad as you imagined it would be.

That being said, some men are downright scared of parenthood. They might even believe that they've got a phobia, and they've got plenty to choose from. There's pedophobia (fear of children), parturiphobia (fear of childbirth), urophobia (fear of urine), scatophobia (fear of feces), and the closely related olfactophobia (fear of odors). There's no specifically named "fear of becoming a father," but the closest we get is papaphobia (fear of the Pope, or is it fear of potatoes?).

Alas, I don't think any of the myriad fears experienced by guys facing fatherhood would qualify as phobias. For one thing, people suffering from phobias are characterized by their avoidance of the thing or situation they fear. And while you may have used every excuse in the book to avoid fatherhood in the past, you're definitely not avoiding it now. Second, phobias are irrational, and fear of fatherhood and everything that comes along with it is definitely *not* irrational.

Learn the Tricks

The steep learning curve of early parenthood provides a great opportunity to learn a lot of tricks and shortcuts to make your life more bearable. One of my favorites is a game I call Diaper Change Chicken. Basically, it's a very subtle move you make to communicate to your wife that you'd be perfectly happy to go

Go to Your Happy Place

If at any time during the first few weeks you find yourself totally lost and be-wildered, there is a place you can go to in your mind. It's an enchanting place where in some ways life is exactly the same as your current situation with the baby. Time has virtually no meaning there, and you find yourself awake at the strangest hours. Just like in your house, the women there have unusually large breasts and can magically bring forth libations as if from the ether. And when-ever you step up to the cloth-covered table, you're taking a chance with craps. That's right, it's Vegas, baby! And while it will be awhile before you can actually go there again, you can take solace in the fact that she'll be there waiting for you when you're ready.

change the baby, but since she's already gotten out of bed, you'll let her do it. Here's how to play: For the first week or so, your wife's maternal instincts will prompt her to voluntarily do much of the baby maintenance. She may even deny your requests to help out (don't get too used to this, because it won't last). During this time, you should observe her very closely. Notice how she pulls back the covers when she gets up to change the baby, and the grunts and groans she makes when it's time for another feeding. Then, as the division of labor gets more equitable, keep an eye out for those indicators. When she reaches for the covers, you make a half-roll toward your side of the bed, and just as her feet hit the floor say, "I'll get this one." If she says, "I'm already up, I'll do it," then you win. You've been honorably discharged from your diaper duties. Keep in mind that you can't play this game forever, but it's fun while it lasts.

You'll also need to figure out the baby's blast zones (see diagram). The inner circle represents an average poop range. Keep in mind that this blast radius continues beneath the baby. The middle circle represents an average male baby's pee range. In accordance with the laws of quantum mechanics, a baby can project pee to more than one place simultaneously. Finally, the outside circle represents the stank range. As noted by the arrows, there is no containing the stank, and no one is safe. Godspeed, my friend.

These early days are also a good time to start figuring out the baby's "tells." Just like a novice poker player will give some indication of what he's thinking—a nervous whistle, finger-tapping, or, in my case, gleeful giggling—your baby will also give you clues as to what's going on. For example, I learned pretty quickly which

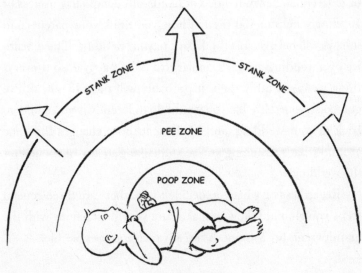

Baby Blast Zones

scrunched-up face indicated a poop and which was for just farts. This may seem insignificant, but at the time it was like deciphering the Rosetta Stone.

Dealing with the Grandparents

Serpentine, Shelly! Serpentine!

—VINCE RICARDO (PETER FALK), *THE IN-LAWS*

Besides the fact that it's from a movie called *The In-Laws,* that quote up there has nothing to do with the subject at hand. I just really wanted to include it in the book somewhere. Seriously, though, you do need to give some thought as to how you're going to deal with the new grandparents. They can be overbearing or deferential, heavy-handed or hands-off, completely useless or amazingly helpful. To predict how you think your parents and in-laws will behave, just think back to your wedding. The dynamics of a wedding are very similar to a baby's arrival, so if everything went smoothly then, it probably will now. If not, you've got to ask yourself what you would do differently if you could go back to your wedding, and implement those changes this time around (that's assuming you're still talking to any of them after the wedding).

Regardless of what you decide to do, there are three general steps you should follow to make sure your interactions with the grandparents are as smooth and advantageous as possible.

1. INSTRUCT THEM

If left unchecked, an overzealous grandparent can transform even the most levelheaded new parent into a foot-stomping, door-slamming teenager. After all, who knows better how to make you feel like a child than your own parents? Laying down the law in this context is a difficult maneuver, since it emphasizes exactly how you're doing things differently than they did. This implies that you think you can do better than they did (which, of course, you do), and that can lead to trouble. But if you feel strongly about this, you have to explain to them that you expect them to do things your way. It's best if you talk to your parents and your wife talks to hers. If your parents disagree with something, tell them that it was your wife's decision and there's nothing you can do about it. Have your wife do the same things with her folks.

2. INDULGE THEM

At some point, though, you just have to let the grandparents run wild with their grandchild. It's their prerogative to occasionally make you crazy, leaving you with an overtired, overfed, and overindulged child. Try not to let it get to you, and definitely don't throw a tantrum. Otherwise you'll get that same condescending admonishment that they used on you when you were twelve.

3. PUT THEM TO WORK

If you can achieve that delicate balance between indulgence and respect, you may reap an invaluable reward. Not only will your relationship with your parents reach a whole new level, but you'll have access to one of the most wonderful gifts that one generation can bestow upon the next: limitless free babysitting, takeout Chinese, and dishwasher unloading.

Back from the Brink

At some point during the first few weeks you're going to reach your wits' end. You're totally exhausted, you want nothing more than just a moment's peace and quiet, and the baby won't eat, won't sleep, and won't stop crying. You get more and more frustrated and angry, until you just want to throttle that tiny little baby. It sounds horrible, like something only a monster would even consider. And yet I can pretty much guarantee that you'll get to that point and you'll have those thoughts, just like every other new father before you. At times like those, it's essential to have a few strategies to bring you back from the brink.

The first thing to remember is that the baby isn't crying just to piss you off. Something's not right, and this is his way of expressing that. Don't take it personally, and don't think it makes you a bad parent (see "How to Survive the Crying Game," below).

Next, try to be there with him in that moment, rather than thinking about what else you could be doing if he would just shut up and go to sleep. It might sound like a cliché, but try counting to ten, and with each number bring yourself from where you want to be to where you are.

One technique that I find particularly helpful is to softly sing a lullaby to the baby, but change the words to express what you're really feeling. The baby won't understand the meaning, he'll just respond to the melody and your tone of voice, and you'll feel better. For example,

Go to sleep, go to sleep.
Won't you please just shut up now.
You are dri-ving me nuts.
I need to go get drunk.

> Or, another favorite:
>
> *Twinkle, twinkle little star.*
> *How I wonder what you are.*
> *Up above the world so high.*
> *If you don't stop crying I'm going to put my head through a freaking wall.*
> *Twinkle, twinkle little star*
> *How I wonder what you are.*

Here's one final thought about those first few weeks. As tough a time as it may be, it's the first phase of your baby's life, and the first one that he'll outgrow. He is about to change more quickly and dramatically than you can imagine, and sometimes it's hard to keep up. In a few short months, you'll have a really tough time remembering anything about those first weeks. You'll look at photographs taken only months before and they'll look as distant as your own baby pictures. So try to hang on to those days if you can. It's a skill that will serve you well moving forward, as you get to times you'll really want to cherish. If, as the baby gets older, you find that you also can't remember those early days, it's probably for the best. That selective amnesia comes in very handy when you start to think about jumping into that full catastrophe all over again with kid number two.

FIRST YEAR TIMELINE

Age	What's Happening	What This Means	What to Do
Newborn	Baby's primary concerns are eating and sleeping.	He'll fit right in at college.	Sleep at work.
1 Month	Baby learns to pacify himself.	Supports the theory that the need for alcohol is not innate.	Prove theory that the need for alcohol spikes in new parents.
2 Months	Baby smiles.	He might actually like you. (Could be gas.)	Smile back (embrace sympathetic flatulence).
3 Months	Baby can express affection.	He's got you wrapped around his little finger.	Keep an eye on your wallet.
4 Months	Baby learns to grab things.	The wholesale denuding of shoulders and armpits, ripped clean by tiny fists of fury.	Always wear closed-collar shirts when holding the baby. Stock up on Bactine.
5 Months	Baby will respond to his name.	He's taken the first step toward eventually ignoring everything you say.	Start counting the days until he moves away to college.
6 Months	Baby can make it through the night without feeding.	There is a God.	Sleep for sixteen days straight to make up for lost time.
7 Months	Baby starts teething.	You'll be swimming upstream against a deluge of drool.	Start sleeping at work again.
8 Months	Baby develops separation anxiety.	A family member actually wants to spend time with you.	Take video; show it to him when he's a surly teenager.

Age	What's Happening	What This Means	What to Do
9 Months	Baby develops sense of object permanence.	He's no longer capable of understanding quantum mechanics.	Hide all snack foods.
10 Months	Baby develops "pincer" grip, between thumb and index finger.	Baby is able to yank out individual nose hairs.	Teach baby to fish olives out from bottom of jar. Make martinis.
11 Months	Imitation.	He'll soon be doing phony phone calls in your voice.	Swear like a sailor around the baby, then just sit back and enjoy.
12 Months	Could start walking.	All hell is about to break loose.	Run screaming.

SEVEN THINGS TO *NEVER* DO AFTER THE BABY ARRIVES

Pregnancy and new parenthood is a crazy time, especially for exhausted, befuddled fathers who have no experience navigating these dangerous waters. You may think you've got your wife figured out, but I guarantee that a previously unseen, possibly terrifying side of her will emerge at some point during the process. Additionally, after the baby arrives, there's a whole new dynamic to the relationship that will need to be navigated, and you're pretty much driving blind. So here are just a few suggestions to help you avoid some of the more likely land mines.

1. Don't Say Anything Hinting That You Still Believe You Have Any Real Power

At the exact moment when that sperm penetrated that egg, whatever semblance of domestic patriarchy you had established up to that point was obliterated forever. From now on, you're at best third-in-command, so get used to it. Frankly, rather than fighting it, you're better off embracing your newly depleted station in life. For example, now when you go shopping for big-ticket baby items, the salesperson will totally ignore *you* and direct all of his questions and commentary at your wife, as if you didn't exist. They'll assume you are totally disinterested in, and completely ignorant of, any and all baby-related paraphernalia. You may actually find it quite refreshing to have so little expected of you. Let's face it: if there's anything the current political climate has taught us, it's that if you lower expectations far enough, it's much harder to disappoint.

2. Don't Diminish the Importance of Your Wife's Role

After thousands of years of men basically scamming women into believing they're inferior, the one area in which women undeniably hold all the cards is the reproductive arena. You will have ample opportunity to marvel at the female machinery and how it works so brilliantly to create new life, so don't skimp on expressing your awe to your wife, who very often may feel more like an old junker than a new hot rod.

3. Don't Be Too Honest

Sure, honesty is the cornerstone of any good relationship, but a few well-placed half-truths, omissions, and bald-faced lies make up the mortar that holds that cornerstone in place. Hormones, body image, and instincts create a mother mind-set fraught with potential for you to say the wrong thing. So if you sense that the truth will get you in trouble, avoid it. If she asks you how she looks two months after the baby is born, don't say, "You look great, especially compared to how I thought you'd look." Just say, "You look great." When discussing who the baby looks like, even if he looks exactly like you, remember that all of the baby's best features come from your wife. Frankly, even when it's plainly obvious that you're full of crapola, she'll most likely appreciate the effort.

4. Do Not Take Your Wife Literally

Throughout the pregnancy and early motherhood, your wife will be riddled with hormones effecting her mood, outlook, and opinion of you in often shocking, humiliating ways (even more so than what you've grown accustomed to). It's very important that you carefully gauge the extent of her insanity and not do anything to incur her wrath.

For example, at some point during the pregnancy your wife may say something like, "You may call me an overprotective, dominating bitch for saying this . . ." That does not necessarily mean she actually wants you to call her an overprotective, dominating bitch, particularly not when you're introducing yourself at your first birthing class. Just something to tuck away in the old memory banks.

5. Don't Say, "I'm Doing Everything Around Here," Even if You Are Doing Everything

Parenting does not come as easily or as naturally to fathers as it does to mothers. While men definitely have an instinct for parenting, it is not as sophisticated and powerful as it is in women. That's not to say that men can't be great parents, just that it may take more conscious effort to do so. This may prompt some poor, misguided fathers to do something of questionable intelligence, namely to believe that they are doing more of the work of parenting than they actually are. A sizeable subset of this group may then go on to do something terrifically stupid: actually express that belief to their wives.

For example, one husband I know was asked by his wife, who was breastfeeding at that very moment, if he would get her a glass of water from the kitchen. He found it necessary to say to his wife, mother of his child who, I may have mentioned, *was breastfeeding at that very moment,* "I'm doing everything around here." Miraculously, he still has all his teeth.

6. Don't Confuse Your Baby with Your Pets

I realize this may be difficult during one of those episodes of extreme mental debility that frequently mark early parenthood, but try your best to never call your baby by your pet's name. Additionally, don't use any of the cute whistles or calls you use with your pets when you're trying to get the baby's attention. While they may be perfectly effective, sometimes disturbingly so, your wife may take offense if you get too comfortable treating her child like a Pomeranian.

7. Don't Ask What She's Doing to That Poor Baby

Has your wife ever been driving the car when something went wrong with the engine, like a fan belt breaks or the AC stops working? I'll bet these are your exact thoughts: *Gee, these sorts of things never happen when I'm driving. I'll bet she did something stupid to cause it.* I'm also assuming you didn't share these thoughts with her, at least not more than once. (If you did tell her a second time, I'm glad you found a second wife with whom to procreate.) There is a parenting analog to this scenario, which demands the same restraint.

As a man, you're likely to take a much more tactical approach to parenting than your wife will. In moderation, this can be an effective complement to your wife's more emotional, nurturing approach. Overstep your bounds, though, and she'll slap you down quicker than a dyspeptic dominatrix. As with a pregnant wife, a baby will often exhibit signs that something's not right, usually expressed as crying. And as with a wife, this does not mean that the baby is "broken" and needs fixing by you, particularly when your wife is holding said baby at the time.

You may think to yourself, *What is she doing to that poor baby?* Do not speak that question out loud, even as a joke. I can guarantee she will not laugh, and will infer a subtext to your question implying that she has done something to cause the crying, and you're just the guy to fix it. It's the same as with the car problem, only in this case you can't get away with sharing your thoughts even once.

My advice, rather than giving your wife a chance to misinterpret your innocent offer of assistance, is to just ask, "Is there anything I can do to help?"

HOW TO CHANGE DIAPERS: THE TAMING OF THE POO*

 Difficulty   *Reward*

"You know how to put these things on?"
"Well, around the butt and up over the groin area."
"I know where they go, old-timer, I just want to know whether I need to use pins or fasteners."
"Well, no, they got those tapettes already on there. It's self-contained and fairly explanatory."

—*from* Raising Arizona

The concept and the reality of poop are so ubiquitous in new parenthood that the simple act of changing a diaper hardly seems to scratch the surface of this gamy domain. Before I became a father I had no direct experience with infantile defecation. I had never changed a diaper in my entire life. I had never even witnessed a diaper being changed, but I assumed that life with a baby was basically a ceaseless onslaught of horrific poops and gruesome diaper changes. Babies to me were simply giggling, oblivious digestive tracts with pudgy ankles. I had no idea what to expect. And as you know, the anticipation of something

---

*Interestingly enough, one of the earliest known uses of the word *diaper* appeared in Shakespeare's *The Taming of the Shrew*. In this instance, though, the word referred to a type of fabric (usually linen), rather than its vital use.

unknown—like IRS audits or casseroles—can scare the . . . well . . . you-know-what out of you.

What knowledge I did have of diaper duty I learned from television. I realize this is difficult to believe, but once again it appears as if the popular media have been less than completely accurate in their depiction of parenthood. We've already discussed how they deal with birth and newborn babies (see "How to Remain Conscious During Delivery"); now we'll take a look at how they deal with diapers. There are two major misrepresentations:

1. While every once in a while your baby will exhibit perfect timing and pee/poop the moment you remove his diaper, it's hardly a daily occurrence. Although when it does happen, you may catch the devilish glint in his eye that gives you the distinct impression that the kid has been holding it in for hours, just waiting for that moment.

2. Some media representations would suggest that not only do some parents find the smell of their child's poop not only unobjectionable, but actually pleasant. While it is true that early on, breastfed babies do produce poop that is inoffensive and some parents may even enjoy it (the way some people like the smell of gasoline), overall, baby poop is among the nastiest odors you'll ever experience (see Poopularity graph). Plus, it lingers, sticking in the nasal passages and upholstery like whitefish at the Friar's Club (see molecular diagram). In short, any experienced parent who tells you that they like the smell of their baby's poop is full of crap (so to speak).

What Is Poopularity?

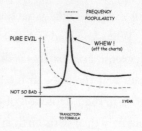

This graph shows the daily frequency and offensiveness, or "poopularity," of baby poop over time. Poopularity is determined using a complex algorithm including:

1. Volume—Does the magnitude befit (in ascending order) a pygmy hippo, Green Bay Packers fan, full-size hippo, Green Bay Packer?
2. Consistency—To what extent is it indistinguishable from creamed spinach?
3. Stank quotient—Measured on a scale ranging from eye-watering to nostril-corroding.
4. Shock value—To what extent will memories of the experience taint your dreams? For example, has the poop advanced to completely cover the baby's back, such that from behind he looks just like George "the Animal" Steele?

Assuming the baby is breastfed at first, you'll notice that there is a very high poop frequency early on, but the smell just isn't that bad. When the baby transitions from breast milk to formula, you may notice a slight change in pungency. We cannot confirm just how great the change is, because the SQ scale isn't calibrated high enough to analyze the data. We lost three good researchers just getting what data we could.

On the right we see a representation of an air molecule just minding its own business and having a grand old time. Then along comes the poop stank, which envelops the air molecule, leaving it despondent and borderline suicidal. What's worse, this malaise seems to last forever, turning the air into the molecular equivalent of the Democratic Party. If you thought cobalt-thorium G had a long half-life, it's nothing compared with the persistence of poop.

But when all is said and done, changing diapers just isn't that bad, and it's certainly not something that requires any formal instruction. After you change your first diaper, you'll be an old pro. As far as dealing with the gross factor, you'll just have to trust me that while it may seem way too disgusting to bear, when you're dealing with your own child and you're fully immersed (sometimes almost literally) in the whole experience, it just becomes something you do (like shaving or avoiding *Sex and the City* reruns). Of course, that doesn't mean we can't find ways to make the whole thing more bearable.

Besides, what choice do you have? Like dancing at a wedding or apologizing for something you didn't do, changing diapers is one of those things you're going to have to do in the end anyway (no pun intended), so let's figure out a few ways to minimize the pain and maximize your brownie points (pun somewhat intended).

1. Follow Her Lead

You're entering the pure womanly domain of nurturing baby maintenance here. The worst thing you can do is show her up. Either she'll make sure you know the mechanics of diaper changing, or when the moment feels right you can ask her to show you how. Your strategy here is to plead total ignorance (this is one of the few times in married life when you're allowed to do so) and let her take the lead. A good place to start is by holding your baby in your outstretched arms, or better yet, tucked under your arm like a football. Then give her the same dumfounded expression you give the waiter at the Chinese restaurant when he asks if you'd like to try the steamed tofu with broccoli. She'll grab the baby away from you, and you're on your way.

2. Be Eager to Learn

You absolutely must enter into this endeavor with the same blissful zeal as when you first learned to throw a Wiffleball or shotgun a beer. Actually, a beer might not be such a bad idea at this juncture.

3. Behold, the Miracle of Poop!

When on diaper-duty, you're the Crocodile Hunter of Ca-Ca, the David Attenborough of Doodie. While you're changing a diaper, enthusiastically announce to your wife all of the wonders of nature that you're privileged to witness. Say things like, "What a big poop! Daddy is so proud of you," "It made it into your hair, that's so wonderful," "Come here, honey, I've never seen this color before," or "Get the tape measure, I think we have a new personal best in projectile pooping." You get the idea.

4. Perfection Is in the Eyes of Her Girlfriends (and Her Parents)

No matter how much you hate changing diapers (and as I said, it's just not that bad), when her friends or parents are over, there's nothing you'd rather be doing on that sunny Saturday afternoon.

If the baby needs changing, you insist that the ladies remain seated and continue downing those Mint Milanos like a pack of voracious hyenas while you gleefully whisk the baby away. When the in-laws are in town, just assume that you're on permanent poop patrol. Doing so can earn you some serious brownie points, while not doing so can earn you a crapload of scorn.

5. Work on Your Breathing

Holding your breath is the best way to render any diaper change minimally disgusting. Some might suggest that you just breathe through your mouth, but I find that doesn't work for me. The smell still gets through, and the thought of those poop-encased air molecules lodging on my palate may be worse than the smell itself. So your best bet is to maximize the amount of time that you can keep those poop-stank barbarians at bay.

First, the better shape you're in, the longer you can hold your breath. So follow the cardio suggestions in the Fit Father section, and that should help.

Second, understand the biology involved. As you might learn in a scuba course, when you're holding your breath the urge to breathe comes not from a lack of oxygen, but from a buildup of carbon dioxide. The increase in acidity in the blood is what tells the brain it's time to breathe again. So there are a couple of things you can do to increase your safe changing time. First, hyperventilate a bit, taking a few fast breaths. This will decrease the acidity in the blood and allow you to go a bit longer without air. Second, when you just can't hold your breath any longer, remember that the buildup of carbon dioxide is the problem, and exhale it all away. This will buy you a few more seconds, plus it might create enough of a breeze to redirect the odor just far enough away.*

Disposable Heroes

I consider myself quite the environmentalist, and while I'm willing to take appropriate measures when it comes to buying a car (Prius), recycling (everything), and experiencing liberal guilt (constant), I'd heard too many horror stories to give even a moment's consideration to cloth diapers. Landfills be damned, I was perfectly happy to embrace the modern (if not environmental) marvel that is the disposable diaper. And I assume virtually all other fathers-to-be feel the same way. Few things frighten men so much as the prospect of several years of changing diapers, and any technological assistance available in that epic struggle will be gleefully embraced.

But I must pass along one piece of advice that I wish I'd been given before we had the baby. When the baby is a newborn, particularly if he's breastfed, the poops are particularly conducive to cloth diapers: they're frequent, not too voluminous, and only mildly offensive. So, for at least a few weeks, you may want to consider using a diaper service, and then switching over to disposables once the noxious deluge really kicks in.

---

*SAFETY TIP: These suggestions, while potentially useful, are provided for comedy purposes only. If you do try them, completely at your own risk, of course, remember to always strap the baby onto the changing table, just in case he decides to try and roll off or, more likely, in case you pass out due to lack of oxygen combined with overabundance of stank.

HOW TO SURVIVE THE CRYING GAME

Difficulty 𝄠𝄠𝄠𝄠 *Reward* 🍺🍺🍺

All babies cry. It's completely normal and natural, but sometimes it's also the single most maddening sound you'll ever hear. And sometimes there's absolutely nothing you can do about it. Crying tests the patience, resolve, and sanity of a new parent more than anything else. Here are a few pointers to help you deal with the inevitable:

1. Seek Help

There's a great little book that has been the salvation of many a new parent. *The Happiest Baby on the Block* by Harvey Karp offers up a simple set of techniques to soothe a crying baby. While it may only work for a few weeks or months, it almost always does work, and it will dramatically improve your life as a new parent. By the way, the techniques are all pretty simple, and since they'll probably only be effective for a short time, I'd recommend just borrowing the book from a friend or getting it from the library.

2. Empathize

First of all, babies hardly ever cry just to piss you off (that'll come later). They may be hungry, scared, or uncomfortable, or they may be crying to get your attention. While the crying may inevitably *result* in pissing you off, you may find it helpful to remember that that wasn't the baby's primary objective.

Since there's no way to stop crying for good, you'll need to figure out a way to live with the wailing. For starters, really try to empathize with what the baby is going through. For the first few months of his life, crying is pretty much his only means of communication. He'll cry all the time to express any number of needs and emotions, whereas fathers, by contrast, tend to cry only at the most emotionally traumatic moments (such as a Game Seven defeat or prostate exam). We can't understand how a baby who isn't horribly traumatized could be so upset. In most cases the baby isn't nearly as upset as he sounds to the father, he's just expressing himself the only way he can. If you can put yourself in his tiny little shoes, you may appreciate his situation a bit more and understand his motivation. I hope that will help ease your frustration.

3. Accept It

A crying baby does not make you a bad parent. If anyone gives you a hard time about your baby's crying, make sure you've got a few choice words for them (see "How to Tell Pushy Parents Where to Stick Their Advice," below).

4. Translate

People will say that you'll be able to translate your baby's cries and know exactly what he's trying to say. I believe that to be the case, but I would suggest that the different cries (for hunger, pain, tiredness, diaper change, insecurity) are really just variants on the same theme: "I own you, be-atch!"

5. Don't Fight It

You know how they say, "A watched pot never boils?" Well, a watched baby never stops crying (OK, he'll stop eventually, but it will seem like forever). My advice to you, especially in the middle of the night, is to just give in and get up. If you try and ignore the baby and go back to sleep, he'll wait until you just doze off and then start up again. But if you grab a book and start reading and, even better, challenge him to keep on crying, he'll stop before you know it. On a related note, if you desperately try to get back to sleep, and then finally give in and decide you'll get out of bed and go soothe him, I guarantee that the moment you approach the door to his room, he'll fall sound asleep (in this case, you can interpret his *silence* as, "I own you, be-atch!").

6. Embrace *Schadenfreude*

Schadenfreude is a word from German meaning to take pleasure in the suffering of another. To put it bluntly, there is no sweeter music to a new parent's ears than the sound of someone else's kid crying while their own baby slumbers silently.

HOW TO FIND EVERYTHING FUNNY (EVEN THE REALLY GROSS STUFF)

Difficulty   *Reward*

Besides the possibility of sending you into a deep dark funk, having a baby also provides limitless comedic potential. The key is to realize that you're going to laugh about all this eventually, so why not start right away? For example, as we waited to board a cross-country flight recently, our son finished two full jars of baby food (green beans and turkey with rice), which boded well for the chances of a peaceful flight. No sooner had we reached a comfortable cruising altitude than he gleefully dug into a bag of rice crackers (his favorite). He must've gotten a crumb stuck in his throat because he started into his standard guttural retching, like a cat working on a hairball. I hope you don't think I'm cruel, but I couldn't help but find this very funny. This time, though, the boy exacted his revenge by hurling a free-flowing spew of the aforementioned baby food all over my shirt, pants, and in-flight meal (which up until that point I didn't think could be any less appetizing). Now *that's* funny.

Another rich source of humor is the marked regression in language usage (actually, it's amazing that you'd even notice the difference, given that most of us are pretty far down on the scale to begin with). As much as you may try to deny it, you'll be drawn into a vast array of baby talk, and the content of your discussions will be dominated by poopies and poopie-related subject matter. Not to worry, though, since another interesting side effect of parenthood is an increased immunity against public embarrassment. It's the wondrous balance of nature.

One related language change is that many seemingly innocuous phrases will suddenly find new and hilarious meanings within the context of parenthood. Here are just a few examples:

- What a little stinker.
- It's all shits and giggles.
- He's always putting his foot in his mouth.
- It smells like ass in here.
- He's sleeping like a baby (waking up every two hours, soiled and soaked).

- He just loves licking that carpet.
- What a pisser.
- He's got money coming out the ass (a few hours after swallowing some loose change).
- That was the single most disgusting (or embarrassing, terrifying, rewarding, hilarious) experience of my life.
- I'm completely pooped.

HOW TO RELIEVE POSTPATER DEPRESSION

Difficulty   *Reward*

The birth of your first child is cause for celebration, an opportunity to marvel at the miracle of life and to bask in the glow of innocence and pure potential. Right? Well, sort of. It's also a possible antecedent to a crippling depression. With the exception of your fortieth birthday, there's nothing like fatherhood to bring on a monstrous, yawning midlife crisis.

The most obvious cause of this particular meltdown is, of course, that you're now a father, just like your father and his father before him. You've got responsibilities, uncertainties, and fears you've never had before. And at times you don't know if the crying will ever stop or when you'll get a full night's sleep again. And, oh yeah, fatherhood means you're old! I don't care how old you actually are or how old you feel, when you have a child, you're old. After all, what do you think of when you think of a father?

Probably someone much, much older than you. Someone who's more like, I don't know, *your* father's age. Well, I've got bad news for you: everyone younger than you, especially those without kids, thinks you're old. And you've just added one more name to the bottom of that list who someday, not too long from now, will think of *you* when he thinks of a father/geezer.

But all that's just the depression talking. In reality, it's not that bad. Postpater depression is very much just a result of the transition you're going through. You'll adjust, but the more you fight it, the harder it will be. One way to help with the transition is to employ the technique I used to deal with turning thirty. I figured that when I was twenty-nine, I was "the oldest among the young." When I turned thirty, I was happy to think of myself as "the youngest of the old." Sure, it sucks to be old, but there'll always be somebody older, and at least you're not him.

The other big cause of postpater depression is the astounding velocity with which a baby changes, and just how imminent that makes the onset of old age seem. The baby changes so quickly, it feels as if your own aging has been shifted into warp speed. You'll think to yourself, "If this kid has developed this much in just a few weeks, it'll only be a matter of months before he'll be a surly, pot-smoking teenager who mocks my music and steals my booze. And just a few short years after that he'll be as old as I am now, and I'll be a doddering old fool."

You may have felt a similar twinge of anxiety when you got married (the whole " 'til death do us part" thing). But in that case you were probably about the same age as your wife (Mr. Trump and Mr. Douglas, you may skip this section), and you'll age together at about the same pace, such that you'll hardly notice it happening. With the kid, as soon as you begin to imagine him as an adult, you invariably imagine yourself as a corpse. But relax, all that's a long, long way off. Just how long? Let's do a little mental exercise to show you just how long you've got before you'll actually be an old man.

When your kid is about six months old and starts to interact with the world, take a close look at that world. The Internet is everywhere; we have DVRs, iPods, and hybrid cars. Then think about what the world was like when you were six months old. For me, that was late summer 1969: it was Vietnam, Woodstock, and the moon landing. As far as I could tell, the entire world existed in black and white. It was an eternity ago. So when you think about how long it will be before your kid looks back at the present time, you can relax a bit. It's a lifetime away.

Another way to think of it is that by the time your kid is the age you are now, you'll have lived exactly as long again as you've lived so far. That's a lot of living. Granted, the next lifetime probably won't be quite as much fun as the last one, but on the positive side, you won't have to go through puberty again and for much of the time you'll be an old fart who just won't give a crap.

So you're not a kid anymore, and some pimply teenager at the grocery store calls you "sir" and asks if you need help with your bags. And your kid will soon grow up to think that you're so much older than him, just as you thought that your father was so much older than you. If that starts to get you down and you think your life is over, your best years are behind you, and you're turning into your father, remember that becoming a father also affords you a certain unwavering disdain for anyone who makes you feel old. Repeat after me: "What the hell do they know, they're just kids." Feels pretty good, eh?

Here are a few other things to think about whenever you get the fatherhood blues:

If you feel the pressure of responsibility, that probably means that you're responsible. You should take solace in the fact that you're not a total screw-up, and that you'll do right by the kid.

If you're feeling old, remember that babies have a remarkable way of making you feel carefree and young. Embrace their innocence and curiosity. Take a few minutes to see the world through their eyes, and you'll probably feel much better.

Remember that having a kid also gives you license to act like a complete idiot whenever you want. If you feel like a kid yourself and you're worried you'll set a bad example, realize that empathizing with your baby is a great way to connect with him and build a strong and lasting bond. So go ahead and burp, fart, and do just about anything else that makes you giggle.

If you feel like time is going way too fast, keep in mind that parenthood just keeps getting better and better. Sure, your baby is growing and changing, but it's just a matter of time before you'll be helping him with his homework, watching him play sports and music, and getting him to do your chores.

Finally, if you ever have any doubt that someday soon you'll be totally thrilled to be a father and you won't trade it for anything in the world, don't worry. Don't just take my word for it (or the word of every other father you could find). Studies (real ones) show that the more involved the father, the greater the reward in better health, more happiness, and higher self-esteem. Just try to be patient.

Look Alive

It's also quite possible that what feels like depression is actually just exhaustion. Spending every waking moment in a haze of drowsiness can be pretty awful and could have serious negative consequences, especially if you have to go back to work soon after the baby is born. For example, during an important meeting you might suddenly doze off in a co-worker's cleavage. Your buddies at work would find it hilarious, but your ersatz pillow might protest. This is just one of many possible exhaustion-induced scenarios to which you might fall victim. I suggest you do everything you can to remain at least adequately conscious during normal business hours.

First of all, use caffeine wisely. I hope that over the past several months you have lowered or eliminated your intake of caffeine. These days, when you truly need it, try to use smaller amounts throughout the day, rather than a double-grande caffe latte in the morning and then another after lunch. Studies have shown that distributing your intake of caffeine throughout the day is more effective in helping you feel alert.

While it will make you feel more alert, caffeine does nothing for your fragile mental state. I have found that meditating for even just a few minutes each day can really refresh your mind and help you think more clearly.

Moving your workout to the morning can help you stay energized all day. You're probably going to be awake before dawn most mornings anyway, so why not make the best of it?

Watching your diet can also help you stay awake. Try to avoid big meals, and keep some healthy snacks like nuts or fruit around to keep you from getting hungry throughout the day. Also, remember to drink plenty of water.

If all else fails, tuck under your desk for a quick afternoon nap. The Spanish have been taking siestas for generations, and since you're now keeping the same hours as a Barcelona socialite, you should give it a try.

HOW TO BECOME A ZEN MASTER DADDY

Difficulty   *Reward*

I have always been an impatient person, but compared to my wife I'm like the Buddha, silently awaiting enlightenment for years beneath the bodhi tree. My wife is so impatient, she got morning sickness during conception. I can't complain, though, since her impatience frequently prompts her to utter the five words every man dreams of hearing after sex: "What took you so long?"

Yet in her role as a mother my wife is supremely patient. She can quietly coax a fussy baby to take his bottle for what seems like an eternity, while I cower in the next room doing my best imitation of Edvard Munch's *The Scream.* That to me is the single most incontrovertible piece of evidence that women are more predisposed to nurturing and caring for their children than men.

I am in awe that my wife—who once couldn't wait to get back from the store, so she tried on her new Victoria's Secret Very Sexy Infinity Edge push-up bra in the car (and she was driving!)—could face with complete calm and resolve every challenge presented by our typically demanding baby. I have challenged myself to try to become half as patient as my wife, and have come up with some suggestions that may help other fathers facing the same predicament.

1. One Thing at a Time
First of all, I imagine every new father asks himself, "Where will I possibly find the time to take care of a baby and have even a

moment left over to catch my breath?" Most of us feel as if our lives are pretty full even before a baby is added to the equation. Even if we give up every moment of peace in the day to the baby, he'll still require more time. So most guys come up with a seemingly brilliant but ultimately ill-fated solution: multitasking.

Multitasking can work great when you're at work, but it's not a good strategy for parenting. For one thing, you'll immediately discover that your baby is not completely under your control. And anytime the baby senses you need him to cooperate so you can get something else done, he'll learn that flinging poop isn't just for primates. To be a better parent, and to more fully enjoy your time with the baby, try your best to set everything else aside. Otherwise, you'll find that parenting becomes just another chore, like mowing the lawn or washing the dog. And definitely don't try to do anything really foolish, like write a book,

Don't Just "Sit" There

One of the keys to becoming more patient with your child is to be as wholly present as possible when you're spending time with the baby. I've often noticed a habit among many fathers that really impedes their ability to do that, namely thinking of themselves as the "babysitter" when they're in charge of the kid.

By definition, when you're spending time with the kid, you're parenting. Don't belittle that time, because I guarantee that it's really important to both your child and your wife. Even though at times you may feel like just a babysitter, you'll always be much, much more. If you don't speak of yourself as a babysitter, you're less likely to think of yourself as one, and more likely to embrace your true role as a father.

while parenting, or you'll put on ten pounds, develop the halt-
ing gait of a cranky old codger, hit the bottle with a vengeance,
and end up baring your soul in a late-night confessional to your
only true friends: Fozzie Bear, Elmo, and a purple octopus-type
thingie.

2. Just Be

OK, so you've tried to unitask with the baby, but you still find
yourself stressed out thinking about all the other things you need
to do before getting your requisite forty-five minutes of sleep
each night. To learn how to get over this tendency, let's tap into
the wisdom of an authority on living in the moment who is right
there in front of you: your baby. That's right, babies are Zen mas-
ters at living in the moment. Of course, that often causes them to
drive us crazy with their constantly shifting demands, but it's also
what allows them to show us what is truly valuable in life.

Babies just are. They're not hung up on the past or the future.
If they're happy right now, then they're happy. If not, all hell
breaks loose. As adults, we would never be able to live that way all
the time, although if it was socially acceptable to start bawling
and/or pooping whenever the mood struck, the world would be a
much better place. But every once in a while, living in the moment can be just the refreshing mental pick-me-up you'll need to
fully appreciate your baby and yourself.

Meditation is basically a mental exercise to train your brain to
live in the moment. The more able you are to stay in the present
moment as you meditate, the better you'll become at being present with your baby, regardless of whether he's being a darling or
a terror. Here's a very quick introduction to basic meditation
practice:

1. Sit upright in a chair with your feet on the floor and your hands resting on your legs. Keep a dignified posture, but stay relaxed.
2. You can close your eyes, or focus on a point in front of you.
3. Breathe in through your nose down to your belly (diaphragmatic breathing), such that your chest doesn't expand but your belly moves outward. Follow the breath with your mind's eye as it enters through your nose and travels down into your lungs.
4. Exhale fully through your mouth, continuing to follow the breath as it leaves your body.
5. Focus on your breathing. When other thoughts enter your mind, acknowledge them and then let them go, returning your mind to your breathing.

The Zen Master Daddy

At first you may want to just see if you can do ten breaths without getting distracted by other thoughts. If another thought breaks through, acknowledge it, let it go, and then start counting again. Eventually, try to lengthen your meditation to five minutes, fifteen minutes, and beyond. To learn more about meditation, read Jon Kabat-Zinn's wonderful book *Full Catastrophe Living*.

In fact, meditation and living in the moment can help you recapture some of that time you thought you'd lost when the baby arrived. If you think about it, your life is made up of countless moments. At any given moment you could be working, relaxing, parenting, sleeping, fishing, and so on. You may consider some of those moments to be better than others (working vs. fishing, for example), but the reality is that every moment is exactly equal to every other moment, and together they all add up to your life. So rather than thinking that you need to finish changing that diaper before you can do what you really want to do, try to be present with your baby while changing his diaper, and appreciate that moment for what it is: as significant a moment in your life as any other moment.

And remember, today's nuisance may be tomorrow's fond memory. I can guarantee that as hard as raising a baby may seem at the time, in the very near future you'll look back on those times as some of the greatest moments of your life. So try your best to enjoy and appreciate those moments when they're happening. I realize how difficult that can be much of the time, but just trying can make things much more bearable.

While I realize that Woody Allen is probably not the best person to go to for parenting advice, he once said something about life that I feel speaks particularly well to the first months of parenting: "Life is full of misery, loneliness and suffering—and it's all over much too soon." I wouldn't say that there's any misery or loneliness in early parenthood, and it hardly produces any true suffering, but it can certainly be a pain in the ass. And it's *definitely* over much too soon.

HOW TO TELL PUSHY PARENTS WHERE TO STICK THEIR ADVICE

Difficulty 🍼 *Reward* 🍺🍺🍺🍺

Did you ever notice how every time you went to the car dealership, the salesperson usually directed the conversation to you, and when he did speak to your wife, he usually treated her like a slow-witted eight-year-old? Well, guess what, when it comes to parenting, the outside world views you as a slow-witted eight-year-old, and treats you like one whenever it sees fit to offer unsolicited advice on exactly how you should be parenting better. Yes, it's offensive and annoying, but if you've ever in your life condescended to anyone about anything, no matter how much they may have deserved it (I'm thinking salesgirl at a snotty fashion boutique or an egotistical supermodel wannabe), you're just going to have to chalk this one up to karma. But that doesn't mean you have to sit back and take it.

One of the best things about fatherhood is that you have absolute license to tell anyone and everyone who butts into your business exactly where to stick their unsolicited advice. That doesn't mean you should go strutting down the street looking for a fight (although it is a great feeling just to know that if anyone messed with your kid you're wholly justified to pound on them like Sean Penn on a Pentax), but you should definitely have some kickass comebacks at your disposal for when someone gets all up in your grill.

If your baby is cranky or crying, and someone tells you what you should do about it:

> *"Don't worry, he'll be fine once he sobers up."*

If someone comes up and touches the baby without asking you if it's OK:

> *Turn to the baby: "Don't worry sweety, ugly/stupid isn't contagious."*
> *Or,*
> *To the toucher: "Ooh, I hope you had pelican pox as a child. 'Cause if not, you've got it now. You should probably call your doctor immediately. Sorry."*

For general backseat parenting from a woman:

> *To the advisor, sincerely: "Thank you so much for the advice."*
> *Then, to the baby, audibly: "You see, honey, you should always show respect to the elderly."*

If someone comments that your baby isn't developing as quickly as he should be:

With a complete straight face and somber tone: "Yes, well, he is retarded, so we've just had to lower our expectations. But thank you for noticing."

And just in case you can't think of anything to say, you can always fall back on the old classic:

"Oh, go f$%& yourself!"

Just in case any of this is misinterpreted someday, I'll drop a few shekels in the therapy jar.

GET A LIFE, AGAIN

*Making the Best of
a Dad Situation*

As your child's first birthday speeds into view, you'll no doubt face a bit of a dilemma. On the one hand, you are now an experienced parent who can face just about any crisis with aplomb and resolve. On the other hand, you're still basically the same clueless dolt you were before the kid arrived. It may seem impossible to reconcile those two contradictory sides of yourself, and it is. The solution, then, is to stop trying to reconcile them. Probably the single greatest secret of successful parents is that you can simultaneously be an excellent parent while being an unadulterated buffoon. The trick is to compartmentalize (and for the love of God, don't let your kids see your dark side until they're old enough to drink away the shame).

When I get together with my college friends, all of whom now have kids, it's really quite surreal. By day we're responsible, mild-mannered parents with good kids we're all trying to raise right, and by night we're back in college again, with all of the requisite idiocy you'd expect.

I remember when one of these friends and I were freshmen years ago, we were walking down the main street on campus and he hip-checked me into oncoming pedestrian traffic. An upperclass-man turned and scoffed. "You're such freshmen," she said. "Yeah," my friend replied, "but we'll still find this funny when we're se-niors, so what's your point?" I didn't realize it then, but even now, with a two-year-old kid and a wife for almost eight years, I *still* find that funny. And soon enough my son will, too. It's the circle of life, and one way or another it finds a way to make you laugh.

HOW TO MAINTAIN THE ILLUSION OF CONTROL

Difficulty   *Reward*

No one is more susceptible to an expert's fearmongering than a parent. Fear is in fact a major component of the act of parenting . . . This leads a lot of parents to spend a lot of their parenting energy simply being scared.

—STEVEN D. LEVITT AND STEPHEN J. DUBNER, *FREAKONOMICS*

As an expectant or new parent, you'll often feel like everyone's an expert and everything's to be feared. For example, is a pacifier good or bad? I always thought it was bad, because it meant you'd end up having braces. I don't know where I got that idea, but that's what I thought. Now the data switch back and forth, most recently with a study showing that use of a pacifier dramatically reduces Sudden Infant Death Syndrome. Does that mean you should force your child to have a pacifier? No, but it illustrates that even something as seemingly benign as a pacifier can cause confusion and fear in new parents. So, who do you believe?

I find that many sources—including one notable bestseller that we've already smacked down—spend too much time harping on everything that *could* possibly go wrong. As if pregnancy, childbirth, and parenting aren't stressful enough, books like that will have you waiting around for all hell to break loose, when you'll suddenly find yourself the subject of a tragic made-for-TV movie (cue the sappy music). And these books hardly exist in a vacuum. "Experts" can take the form of doctors, friends, parents, talk show hosts, magazines, and commercial pitchmen. And the fears that parents experience aren't limited to the health of the baby. Societal and marketing pressures are constantly bombarding parents with suggestions that they must do and buy certain things or else they risk depriving their child, with potentially devastating consequences for child and parents alike. It's no wonder that parents so often feel as if they've ceded control of their lives to their babies and the cadre of overconfident "experts." I've got a few suggestions to help you hang on to some sense of control as a new parent.

Control Over Your Baby

There's a brilliant article in the business literature called "On the folly of rewarding A, while hoping for B" by Steven Kerr, which basically states that the world is full of examples where our stated goal is one thing, but the rewards system we put in place promotes the exact opposite. For example, in the sports world coaches always talk about teamwork, but in reality it's the individual stats that earn the scholarships, huge salaries, and notoriety. Or in politics, we see that voters often claim that they want their politicians to make the tough choices, but they actually vote for politicians who offer easy solutions. This tendency also afflicts parents.

No parent enjoys hearing his or her baby cry. Our immediate desire is to soothe the baby, which makes us and the baby feel better. The problem is, we may be reinforcing the very behavior we're trying to stop. Babies cry for many reasons, but one of the more common reasons is to lure the parents in to soothe them. Each time you react to that crying by going into the baby's room and soothing him, you're teaching the baby that crying works to achieve their goal. So you may temporarily stop the crying, but in the long run you're rewarding crying and reinforcing its power (see diagram below). It may sound like an easy problem to correct, but it's not.

Parenting is tough, and it's definitely more of an art than a science. Sometimes you follow your gut and it gets you into even more trouble. Babies are sneaky, manipulative little buggers, and they know all your weaknesses and just how to exploit them. It's easy to fall victim to their wily ways, but with a little help you can consistently learn to outsmart even the cleverest among them.

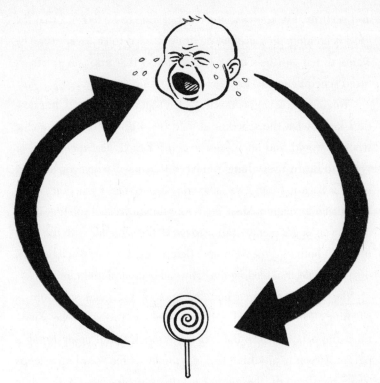

*A treat intended to stop the crying might
actually reinforce the behavior.*

Setting Schedules

Some experts will tell you that babies need structure, while others
will suggest that imposing structure on a baby stifles his creativity
and adventurousness. All I can tell you is that as long as the jury is
still out on which way is better, in my opinion structure wins
hands-down. The main reason is that imposing a structure on the
baby helps establish some predictability in your life. It also seems to
work pretty well for the baby. For example, if your baby comes to
expect that he'll be fed at certain times, it creates a sense of comfort

and security. He knows that it's about time to be fed and that the food is coming, so therefore he doesn't need to cry every time he wants to tell you he's hungry. I've found that imposing a structured schedule makes my life as a parent much easier.

You may be asking yourself, "That's all well and good, but how do I know what the schedule should be? I don't even have a clue where I would find such information." Relax. As I mentioned in "How to Learn Everything You Need to Know," when you actually have the baby in front of you and you need to set the schedule, you'll have that information. Most likely your doctor will tell you how to do it, and you've got plenty of time to tweak the schedule with the baby until you both find the right one. Before you know it, you'll both be on a schedule, and feeding the baby will become a no-brainer.

Besides an eating schedule, the other crucial schedule is sleeping. The quality of a baby's sleep is probably the single most important determinant of how much you'll enjoy being a parent. If you're anything like me, the first time your baby sleeps through the night, in the morning you'll feel like Princess Buttercup emerging safely from the Fire Swamp (perhaps I've revealed too much; better make a donation to the therapy jar).

The point is, getting your baby to sleep through the night is hugely important, and a major challenge.

Perhaps the most surprising thing I learned about newborns during my wife's pregnancy was that they aren't born with the ability to put themselves to sleep. It's something they must be taught how to do. Another surprising bit of information was that "sleep begets sleep," so you can't just exhaust a baby and expect him to sleep through the night. The better they nap during the day, the better they'll sleep at night. I soon discovered that these facts came from the single most important book on parenting that I've read: *Good Night, Sleep Tight* by Kim West and Joanne Kenen. In simple, gentle detail this book explains a tried-and-true method for training your baby how to fall asleep.

I realize that there are lots of different sleep philosophies, from "Ferberizing (just letting babies cry)," to never letting babies cry. West's method is somewhere in between, and worked beautifully for my wife and me. Basically, if you want your baby to sleep through the night, you've got to train him to do so. It's not easy, but when the baby is physiologically able to make it through the night without food, West recommends that you stop feeding him. There's no guarantee it will work, but I know if my parents didn't cut me off when I was a few months old, I'd still be waking up screaming at 3:00 A.M. and jamming it to the fridge to graze on a leftover meatball parm.

All of this is to say that in my opinion both parents and baby are better off with consistent, compassionate parenting controls in place. It may not be easy at first, and you may struggle with it for months, but eventually you'll all be better off. And you can get some sleep.

Control Over Your House

It's remarkably easy to allow your house to be overrun with baby toys and supplies. If you've established some semblance of control over your life and your baby, you've gone a long way to controlling your house as well. There are a few other important points and strategies to keep in mind as well.

I have a friend who teaches marketing at UCLA. One Sunday afternoon he was watching television with his six-year-old son when a commercial for some toy came on. The boy looked up at his father and said, "Daddy, do I want that, or are you making me want that?" Smart kid. You'd be well advised to remember that question every time you think you want or need something for the baby. The fact is, we live in a consumerist society, and only hormone-ravaged teenagers are more coveted by product-peddling marketers than new parents. If you thought the Matrimony Industrial Complex was scary, just wait until you find yourself immersed in the Reproduction Industrial Complex.

I mentioned at the beginning of the book that you'd have no trouble learning everything you need to know about parenting.

You Da Man!

Regardless of how incessant the marketing onslaught is, the ultimate decision-making responsibility lies with the parents themselves. I was at a party a few months back, and I overheard a new father talking about how he absolutely needed to move to a bigger house. He didn't need additional bedrooms, just more space. "People these days have so much stuff for the kids," he said, "it's just ridiculous." *No,* I thought, *it's not people. It's YOU. If you don't want so much stuff, don't buy so much stuff.* Trust me, the kid won't miss any of it. He can live without Baby Uggs. Babies are just like cats and dogs; they get more pleasure from a shoelace, a plastic cup, or the box the toy came in than from the toy itself.

Basically, all it takes is a little education and a little responsibility to regain control, and figure out which stuff you really need and which you don't. Here's an example of how an item might appear to be a necessity, and how you can figure out if actually is, or if it's just marketing:

Somehow, about four months into my wife's pregnancy, we spontaneously came to the realization that the *Baby Einstein* DVDs were just wonderful. We had never seen them, knew nothing about them, and yet we felt they'd be an invaluable asset for our baby. We were drawn inexorably to them with no real understanding of why. We had no control over the urge, as if some nefarious dark force had ensnared us and we had no choice but to succumb to its temptations. I was on the verge of a complete mental collapse, imagining a vast corporate conspiracy to brainwash us and our child, spanning the generations to enlist a consumer army into the service of some giant rodent-like overlord. And then I realized that *Baby Einstein* is owned by Disney, and it all made perfect sense. By the way, our son is doing just fine without those DVDs.

The problem is, most of the time the same people who are trying to teach you something are also trying to sell you something (for example, just because there are dozens of articles on the latest, greatest diaper bags, that doesn't mean you need one. A decent backpack works just fine). You're in a vulnerable position, and they know it. One of my goals is to help new parents become comfortable and confidant enough to distinguish between fear and necessity, and be able to make decisions for themselves, despite what the commercial forces tell them.

Decluttering Strategies

WAIT AND SEE
I suggested earlier that the Just in Time inventory model works well for parenting information. The same is true for most of the stuff you'll buy for your baby. In many cases, you just

don't know what you need until you need it, and if you buy things ahead of time you're likely to get lots of stuff you don't really need.

JUST ONE WORD

When Mr. McGuire took Ben Braddock aside in *The Graduate* and offered his one word of advice, he couldn't have been more right. Any new parent will agree that the world seems to be made of plastic. My advice to you, to help you keep all that plastic from taking over your house, is also just one word: *baskets.* Put baskets everywhere throughout your house, so you can just lob toys, bibs, books, and everything else in there from across the room.

GIVE IT AWAY, GIVE IT AWAY, GIVE IT AWAY NOW

You will not believe the amount of stuff you will accumulate with a new baby. Much of it is necessary, but the incessant avalanche of toys and clothes comes mostly from the fact that people just love shopping for baby stuff. Everything is relatively cheap, and most of it is just as cute as can be. The end result, though, is a house just overrun with stuff. Once you get a sense of what you actually need, I highly recommend aggressive culling of the stock. Set aside a big box for giveaways, and make regular trips to Goodwill, or whichever charity you prefer. You'll not only keep your house from being overrun, you'll also get a nice little tax writeoff.

HOW TO MAKE SURE THE BABY SAYS "DADDY" FIRST

Difficulty *Reward*

Tired of your wife getting all the attention and sympathy? Really, what's all the fuss about? All she did was grow another human being inside her, squeeze it out of her like a cantaloupe through a garden hose, and then proceed to nourish this new life with manna brought forth from two miraculous organs that, until recently, were little more than your frivolously fingered fun-bags. What about you? Where are *your* props? I mean, that car seat didn't install itself!

Be patient, my pretties, and you shall have your sweet revenge. And what better way to avenge a meaningless and minor slight against you than to inflict on the mother of your child a soul-crushing blow that will haunt her for the rest of her life? Plus, it'll keep you giggling for days.

Getting your child to say "Daddy" first is just one of the countless pranks you can pull using your progeny as an unwitting conspirator (see "How to Use the Baby to Get Away with Just About Anything"). And it certainly won't be the last time you'll mess with your child's mind for your own amusement.

Luckily for you, pulling off this prank shouldn't be too hard. First of all, you start out with a 50 percent chance of the kid randomly naming you first. Plus, there's an interesting study by a French linguist suggesting that *Papa* may have been the first words uttered by Neanderthal infants (and with luck your kid will be at least as smart as they were). The theory is based on data showing that *Papa* is a remarkably common word, with a similar definition, across the vast majority of languages. So statistics and history are all in your favor. All that's needed is a little nudge in the right direction to make sure your child complies.

The first thing to do is to express a desire to be called *Papa* as well as *Daddy*. This is more than just a Hemingway fixation; it's a way to greatly increase your chances of getting the kid to perform. Not only does it give you two words to shoot for, but the *p* sound tends to appear much earlier in language development. Since it's formed in the front of the mouth (along with the *m* in Mommy, unfortunately), you're more likely to be called *Papa* before *Daddy*. But for our purposes, either one works.

There are several theories about just how children learn language. None of the theories explain language development completely, but each has its merits. For our purposes, we'll look at just two: Imitation and Reinforcement.

Imitation Theory basically says that children learn to speak by copying what they hear. Obviously, that doesn't cover all language development, but children will often imitate what they hear (which will explain why, in a couple of years, you'll receive an irate call from your child's teacher the day after your team loses the Super Bowl). So whenever you're alone with the baby, be sure to make it clear that you're Daddy or Papa, and that's about the coolest thing ever.

You can also, purely by coincidence, constantly repeat clever sayings that have lots of *p*s and *d*s in them. There's the old classic, "Peter Piper picked a peck of pickled peppers." Then there's the updated version, "Dirk Diggler dunked a dozen Dinky Donuts." You get the idea. Of course, you don't want to do this too much around the wife or she'll get suspicious. And you'll definitely need to make a donation to the therapy jar.

When the whole family is together, you can utilize Reinforcement Theory. Simply put, you want to provide positive feedback to your baby when his babblings include the letters *p* or *d* or sound like *Daddy* or *Papa*. Of course, you want to positively reinforce *all* of your child's attempts at language, but it can't hurt to lay it on extra-thick to achieve your mischievous goals.

When the baby finally names you first, don't forget to record the moment for posterity (after rubbing it in the wife's face with a little baby-loves-me-best dance). I'd suggest making up T-shirts, coasters, and possibly even a few of those twelve-pound etched glass tabletop cigarette lighters your grandparents loved so much to commemorate the occasion. Also, it couldn't hurt to alert the local media.

HOW TO REMAIN SANE WHEN FLYING WITH A BABY

Difficulty   *Reward*

Before I became a father, I imagined that flying with a baby would be, at best, a profoundly awful and traumatic experience, like being trampled by a moose or suffering through another John Kerry presidential campaign. I could almost feel all those leering, baleful eyes upon me as the baby infused the cabin with ear-shattering wails and eye-watering odors. I could see us racing off the plane and up the jetway, trailed closely by a scythe-wielding, torchbearing mob of our fellow passengers.

Before the baby arrived I had always traveled in that gleeful, luminous reality of preparenthood. I napped, I read a book, I watched the in-flight movie. I even joined the mile-high club, albeit on just an individual membership. Whenever a screaming infant would threaten to befoul that perfect little world, I'd be right there alongside all the other passengers, wishing any number of poxes and plagues upon the baby and his parents. I couldn't imagine myself as one of them. And yet here I stand, a living testament to the fact that no flight lasts forever, all babies do stop crying eventually, and you cannot actually die of embarrassment. Here's how I survived my journey to the other side.

1. Plan Tactically

As experienced a flier as you may be, adding a baby into the equation is like tossing a marmot into the bathtub. It's pretty much just absolute mayhem. As with every episode on our little journey, you'll eventually get used to it, but the first couple of trips can be pretty hairy.

PACKING

I hate to be the one to break the news, but your days of traveling with just a carry-on are over. From this moment on, you'll be packing like Paris and Nicole on a six-week bender in Bangkok. And the bags you do carry on will be packed mostly with baby stuff. I would recommend making a list of everything you need and start to pack well in advance of your trip (like today).

Besides the requisite stockpile of baby food and diapers—lots and lots of diapers—you may want to consider adding a few other things to your carry-ons. First of all, Baby Benadryl may be a wonderful mild sedative for a whacked-out baby. Of course, there's a chance that Baby Benadryl may have the exact opposite effect, sending a whacked-out baby into fits of hyperwhackidity. So be sure to do a test run before you travel, and definitely ask your pediatrician before giving your child *any* drugs.

Also, pack a bunch of little toys the baby hasn't seen yet (you may want to raid the local 99-cent store and spend about twenty bucks on little doodads). If you're feeling particularly ambitious, you can even wrap each gift. Then, when the baby gets fidgety on the flight, just whip out a new toy and buy yourself a few minutes of silent fascination. Repeat as necessary until landing.

TIMING

As with every other aspect of your life, flying with a baby is seriously affected by issues of timing. First of all, start flying with your baby as soon as your pediatrician says is okay. It's much easier to travel with very young babies, since they require less stuff, they sleep most of the time, and, most importantly, they're not mobile.

Next, when the baby's a few months older, planning the actual times of your flights becomes important. At this point, babies are not likely to sleep soundly on a plane, so planning flights for after bedtime is probably a bad idea. Try to fly during your baby's normal waking hours, and the likelihood of him napping depends a great deal on how benevolent you were in a previous life.

Finally, to make your life a bit easier, try to avoid jet lag by staying within your own time zone if possible.

TICKETS

To buy or not to buy, that is the question. Most airlines allow children under the age of two to fly for free sitting on your lap, or they will sell you a ticket for your baby at a deep discount (upward of 50%). The biggest dilemma facing new parents is whether to not buy a ticket and risk a full flight forcing you to hold the baby on your lap for the entire trip, or to buy a ticket and risk regretting it when you find out the flight is mostly empty.

For the first couple of months, babies are very small and easily transportable, so I would suggest that you consider not buying a ticket. After that, you'll need to balance your risk tolerance with the likelihood of a packed flight, along with your baby's demeanor. If you're taking your little terror home for Thanksgiving, get a ticket. If you're flying off-peak with a little angel, you could probably save your money. Regardless of when you fly, if you decide to go without a ticket for the baby, try to get a window and an aisle seat for you and your wife, leaving the middle seat empty. As the flight fills up, those seats will be the last to go.

If they fly to your destination, I'd recommend checking out Southwest Airlines. Because of their policy of unassigned seating, you've got a much better shot at having an empty seat for your baby. Think about it: You board the plane first (an unheralded benefit of traveling with a baby) and grab a window seat for you and an aisle seat for your wife, with the baby in the middle. As the other passengers board and look for seats, they are highly unlikely to even get close to you, let alone ask if your baby's seat is available. Not that I would ever recommend you do anything to make your baby cry, but suffice it to say that if he's a little cranky, your chances of keeping that seat are even greater.

2. Act Thoughtfully

If you're afraid of flying (or more accurately, afraid of crashing), there's no more effective distraction than a baby. You'll be so focused on taking care of the baby and not pissing off your fellow passengers, you won't have time to concern yourself with worrisome questions like, "How can this hulking heap of metal possibly stay airborne?"

Are you ever fully comfortable and relaxed while flying? Probably not, so you've got to assume the baby won't be, either. To help the baby out, be sure to have a bottle ready to give during takeoff and landing. This will help the baby clear his ears during the change in pressure, and can also help soothe the baby during these tense times. Also make sure you've got familiar foods and toys at hand to make the baby feel at home.

You'll also need to act thoughtfully toward the other passengers. If the baby does start crying, at the very least you'll need to show the other passengers that you feel their pain. Tend to the baby, make calming sounds audibly enough so the other passengers can hear, and walk the baby up and down the aisles to make it perfectly clear that you're doing everything you can to keep the baby quiet. Another good strategy is to buy a round of drinks or bring along some chocolates with which to mollify the other passengers.

3. Think Relatively

If the baby just won't settle down and you've exhausted all possible strategies, you can find solace in the fact that flying with a baby is just like camping in bear country. Out in the woods, you don't need to outrun the bear, just your fellow campers. And your baby doesn't need to be perfectly behaved on the plane, just better than someone else's kid.

4. Don't Give a Crap

Finally, a surefire solution to this problem is to just not give a rat's ass about what anyone else thinks. Sure, people give you dirty looks and think nasty, sadistic thoughts about you, but who cares? You'll probably never see them again, and so what if you

---

High Anxiety

Here's yet another example of just how pervasively fatherhood can affect your life. Many parents discover, after years of carefree air travel, that they're suddenly terrified of flying. Some may wonder about the cause, but it's obviously the same thing that's causing your back pain, your bald spot, and just about every other chronic ailment: the kid. Rather than feeling frustrated or spiteful that this little creature could turn you inside out so easily, you should keep in mind that baby-induced anguish is really just proof that you're a good parent. In other words, you're a nervous wreck because you care.

Your fear of flying is probably a fear that you may fail to protect your child. You would like to think that you can always keep your baby safe, and in most cases you do so without much thought. But flying raises all sorts of fears, and you may feel that by boarding that plane you're actually putting your child in harm's way. While you may get some sense of reassurance by these thoughts, that probably won't make you any less nervous.

I would recommend that you anticipate the anxiety and try to prepare for it ahead of time. There are many things you can do to alleviate the fear. I often use meditation to help me relax. I focus on my breathing and visualize a perfect place where I used to go swimming on hot summer afternoons. If that doesn't work, there's always Xanax. There are also more drastic measures you might consider. I know parents who, whenever they fly without the kids, always take separate flights. That way, if something happens, their kids won't be orphaned. It might sound like a ridiculous inconvenience, but just wait. Someday it might not seem so crazy.

By the way, you shouldn't necessarily avoid flying alone with the baby. Sure, he'll make your trip much more difficult, but you'll be amazed at how well people treat a father flying solo with his baby. Maybe it's because everyone is impressed with you, or maybe it's because they think you're an idiot and need their help. Either way, if it increases my chances of getting a free upgrade or even a free drink, I'm all for it.

do? And actually, some good may come from the experience. After all, there's hardly a better way to promote population control.

HOW TO PROTECT YOUR STUFF (AND THE BABY, TOO)

Difficulty *Reward*

There are two somewhat contradictory truisms about babyproofing. One is that you've got plenty of time to get it done (at least six months, or just before the baby starts crawling). The other is that there's no such thing as a house being completely babyproof (you just want to make sure that when he does get into something he shouldn't, the consequences are more hilarious than worrisome).

The vast majority of babyproofing measures are completely

intuitive. You need to cover electrical outlets, lock cabinets, put gates on stairs, protect sharp corners, and so on. Beyond that, you can discover many of the less essential measures just by letting the baby crawl around and get into things. Babies are remarkably adept at exposing weaknesses in your deflector shield. This technique will also let you determine which things you don't need. For example, if the baby shows no interest in cranking up the volume or pulling all the knobs off the stereo, you probably don't need to buy a guard to cover it (at least until he does show an interest).

Silence the Squeak

A squeaky hinge or a creaky floor can be an exhausted parent's greatest nemesis. After hours of frantic cajoling, you finally get the baby to sleep, only to have the faintest chirp from a hinge send him once again into hysterical shrieking fits. Do yourself a big favor and take a few minutes to hit all the hinges and latches in the house with silicone spray (not WD-40), which should take care of any squeaks. The floors can be a tougher proposition. If you've got an old house and all of the floorboards creak, you may just need to live with it or hire someone to fix them all. If it's just one or two spots, there are a few tricks you can try. First, try using baby powder, which, ironically, is not recommended for use on babies (the talc is the problem, so instead use powder with cornstarch). Sprinkle the powder over the seam between the offending boards and work it into the crease. That should reduce the friction between the boards and silence the squeak. If that doesn't work, you can also try using a little liquid soap in the seam between the boards. Beyond those quick fixes, there are other strategies, including reinforcing the floor from below or drilling down into the subfloor beneath the carpeting. You should be able to find kits for your particular situation at Home Depot.

There are countless resources for getting all the babyproofing supplies that you'll need. You can either install everything yourself or hire someone to do it. If you decide to do it yourself, I would suggest that once you get your list together, check the "Baby Safety & Health" category on eBay and see what kind of deals you can get (of course, I wouldn't buy anything that's not brand-new).

One issue that I have with the whole babyproofing industry is that it tends to focus exclusively on the safety of the child. Sure, that's important, but it doesn't mean you need to ignore another possible consequence of having a baby in the house; namely, the outright destruction of *your* stuff. I'm going to assume that you'll figure out how to keep the baby away from the laundry detergent and prevent him from bonking his head repeatedly on a sharp-cornered credenza.

You probably haven't given much thought to exactly how you're going to keep the baby from dropping and/or drooling on your most prized possessions. And if you're anything like me, your most prized possessions usually take the form of the latest in high-tech gadgetry. So let's take a moment to make sure you can protect against the old drool 'n' drop. Keep in mind throughout this discussion that protecting your baby or your stuff presents a great opportunity to buy all sorts of semi-useful accessories that you would otherwise have to justify. So whenever you feel like it, go nuts.

Computers

Babies love computers. The image on the screen gets their attention, but what truly fascinates them is the keyboard. It's virtually impossible to type with a baby on your lap, since he'll immediately lean forward and start banging on the svlknsdd;kljdfd;kl (see what I mean). Plus, those tiny little fingers are just perfect for plucking off random letters and command keys. And as you'll no doubt discover, when a baby is fixated on a particular task, his brain becomes incapable of moderating the flow of drool. There must be some law of infant biomechanics that wherever the hand grabs and the eye fixates, the drool will eventually land. Of course, you also need to be wary of the occasional projectile vomit, as well as your own drool for those times when you just need a nap.

There are a few things you can do to protect against these inevitable assaults on your computer. First of all, you may want to install software that will allow you to lock your keyboard. Rixler Software (rixler.com) has a nice little program called Computer Lock Up that allows you to quickly lock your keyboard so you can let the wee sprout go at it.

To protect your keyboard against drool or puke (which gives a whole new meaning to the term *reboot*), consider getting a keyboard cover. If you use a Mac, check out iSkin.com for very cool keyboard covers and protective gear for other Apple products as well.

Fatherhood puts all your electronics at risk.

Cell Phones and Other Gadgets

As I mentioned at the beginning of the book, babies are drawn to cell phones, PDAs, and MP3 players like Rush Limbaugh to hillbilly heroin, so make sure you've got some old decoys around to keep the kid off the scent of your current models. Eventually, though, he's going to get his hands (and mouth) on them, so make sure you've got them protected.

Also, babies love to grab cords and yank whatever they're connected to down to the ground. They seem to be especially fond of the white cords used for so many Apple devices. Be sure to keep cords wrapped up and out of reach, and whenever possible, go wireless.

We recently bought a waterproof case for our digital camera so we could use it while diving or just whenever we're out in wet weather. This little accessory definitely comes in handy around the baby.

You'll also find that babies will always grab for your glasses. This would be fine if it weren't for the possibility of a nasty eye-poke. So to prevent this from happening, you may want to get yourself a pair of Croakies so the baby can grab and play with the glasses and stay safe.

There are a few other things you might want to think about protecting.

The Car

Short of shrink-wrapping every upholstered surface in your car, there's not a whole lot you can do to protect against the inevitable spill or spit-up. You could get a fabric protector or put down seat covers, but ultimately your car will be overrun by toys, Cheerios, and a certain aroma that will forever mark it as first and foremost a baby transport vehicle. As far as I can tell, the only way to truly babyproof your car is to make sure the baby never rides in it. Obviously, the only reasonable solution is to get a two-seater. (By the way, good luck selling that idea to the wife.) And, speaking of the wife . . .

The Wife

That's right, the wife. Remember birth control? Well, it's back, and more crucial than ever. If you thought you wanted to avoid pregnancy when you were young and stupid, you'll *really* want to avoid it when you're young, stupid, and already completely exhausted from the first kid. In fact, you may want to consider a multimethod approach, just to be on the safe side.

HOW TO SEE YOUR WIFE AS A MILF

Difficulty   *Reward*

There's a commonly held misconception regarding sex after the baby arrives, namely, that any number of things can cause disinterest, discomfort, or dyspepsia. The most common concern, I suppose, is that you won't find your wife sexually attractive after you've witnessed childbirth. You'll be happy to know that sex after pregnancy isn't all that different from sex during pregnancy, which isn't all that different from sex before pregnancy. In fact, there may even be some improvements.

They Might Be Giants

For those of you who are concerned that you'll no longer find your wife attractive after you've seen her give birth, I've got three words for you: major-league yabbos. That's right, after countless shocking and profoundly disturbing surprises, here comes the first and possibly only pleasant surprise in the whole epic journey to fatherhood: natural breast enhancement. Your wife will be better endowed than Shiloh Jolie-Pitt's trust fund. Of course, they'll be so tender that you don't get to play with them, but that's a small price to pay for bringing a bit more bodaciousness to the world. And while they won't stay this way forever, eventually you'll be happy to trade off a little size to once again have full visitation rights.

And by the way, to address another concern that I'm sure many of you have regarding any lasting effects below the equator, let me just say that the female body is astoundingly resilient.

The Need for Speed

You might think that there's nothing good that could come from having a baby around who wakes up every couple of hours, but there's at least one thing: your wife will want to get the sex over with as quickly as possible. And it's not because she's disinterested or wants to get back to *Law & Order*, it's just because she's worried that the baby will wake up. First of all, that means you can finally abdicate virtually all foreplay responsibilities with impunity. I'm sure that's an opportunity that even Uncle Junior*

---

*Corrado Soprano Jr., Tony's uncle on *The Sopranos.* Junior once had a fondness for a certain amorous act that his less indulgent compatriots found emasculating (see the first sentence on page 135).

would appreciate. It's really a time to engage in a purely male version of intercourse, the kind that's discussed derisively on daytime talk shows, but which always seems appealing when you see it on Animal Planet.

Select Company

Sure, your wife is now a mother, and motherhood suggests a certain asexual, June Cleaver-like nature. But certain mothers are able to shake off the stultifying mantle of motherhood and embody an allure they didn't have before. Gentlemen, I give you the elusive and beguiling great-breasted MILF. And by virtue of the fact that you won't have sex for weeks after the baby is born, your wife will necessarily join the selective ranks of MILFdom. From Mrs. Robinson to Stifler's mom, MILFs have intrigued eager young males with their smoky maturity, their extensive knowledge of the erotic arts, and their faintly palpable desperation. It's irresistible, and now your wife is one of them.

Of course, you will have to make a few difficult adjustments, including possibly doing the deed with the baby in the room. The innumerable *Penthouse* letters about sex in public notwithstanding, most guys aren't interested in being watched. Sure, it's an easy way for the *Desperate Housewives* writers to kill ten minutes of narrative every week, but most guys (myself included) can't handle the added pressure, the risk of embarrassment, or, in the case of sex within baby range, the profound weirdness of the whole thing. Try it out on the dog first, and see how that goes.

By the way, if anything will be more disturbing to your child than thinking about you having sex before he was born, it's thinking about you having sex afterward. So I've been dumping whatever cash I could get my hands on into the Therapy Jar throughout this entire discussion.

HOW TO GET THAT #%&%$ SONG OUT OF YOUR HEAD

Difficulty   *Reward*

I'm not one to go in for religious dogma, and with the exception of George Lucas's screenplay for *Star Wars Episode I: The Phantom Menace,* I've never contemplated violence against a fellow scribe. But at 2:00 A.M., kept awake for the third straight night by some maddeningly catchy tune—"Rubber Blubber Whale," "C is for Cookie," or "The Cute Little Birdie Whose Song Sears into Your Brain Until You Want to Chisel It Out With an Ice Pick"—I've often entertained thoughts of issuing my own personal fatwah against certain songwriters (especially that crafty sonofabitch Raffi).

    Getting a horrible children's song stuck in your head is definitely among the more common and potentially debilitating afflictions of fatherhood. You're just going about your day, minding your own business, when suddenly there it is, that haunting refrain seeping across your brain and smothering all other thoughts like the blob, "the wheels of the bus go 'round and 'round, 'round and 'round, 'ROUND AND F$%^ing 'ROUND," ad nauseam. I'm actually taking quite a risk just writing this (as you are reading it), since now I've got that song in my head. But I will persevere.

    A song that gets stuck in your head is affectionately called an *earworm,* which is a literal translation of the word the Germans used to describe the phenomenon, *ohrwurm.* James Kellaris, a marketing professor (of course) at the University of Cincinnati, has studied earworms extensively. He describes the process as a kind of "cognitive itch" that can only be scratched by repeating the song in our heads. He has also found that people who are tired, stressed, or particularly neurotic tend to be more susceptible to earworms. Of course, that pretty much describes all new fathers.

So what can we do to exterminate this particular bug? You could try to legislate it away, as New York mayor Michael Bloomberg did when he proposed banning Mr. Softee ice cream trucks from playing their insidious jingles as they troll the streets for portly patrons. It's not such a bad idea, particularly for those poor souls on the busier Mr. Softee routes. But it's hardly a viable solution. If it's not the Mr. Softee theme (which, if you don't know it, is "Pop Goes the Weasel" played on Satan's calliope), it'll be something else. How about a more practical suggestion?

One such idea is to just play the song out in your head until its conclusion. This technique was actually employed by Mozart, who would be driven crazy (even crazier than usual) when his children practiced the piano and left scales unfinished. He'd constantly finish the scales in his head until he could go to the piano and finish the scales out loud. Only then would he get relief from the earworms.

Another possible strategy is to try and distract yourself with a little mental or physical exercise, anything to get your mind onto other things. You could also try to substitute another song, but that's risky because you may just end up with the new song stuck in your head.

When all else fails, try infecting someone else. There's an old

Mark Twain short story in which the author laments having a "jingling rhyme" stuck in his head, and the only thing that will dislodge it is to pass it along to someone else. You really can't lose with this remedy. Either you banish the earworm, or you get a good laugh at someone else's expense. After all, misery loves company (an old adage you may find yourself and your wife clinging to with some frequency).

Finally, if you find you just can't get songs out of your head, at least make them decent songs. It's not written anywhere that babies need to listen exclusively to children's music. When they're very young, it's the basic elements of the music that engage them, not the perniciously cute melodies and lyrics per se. So crank up some Rolling Stones, U2, Fishbone, or anything that'll get you and the wee sprout bopping along. That way the voice ringing out in your head every night at 2:00 A.M. is more likely to be Bono's than Barney's.

Silencing the Evil One

Besides all those addictive melodies, there is another sound that sends otherwise even-tempered new fathers into hysterical fits of rage. I'm speaking, of course, of that googly-eyed giggling bastard Elmo. Not since the Plastic Ono Band has one voice caused so much misery. It's time to silence the beast, so that new fathers everywhere can once again play among the children without fear of suffering a sudden Elmo-induced aneurysm.

First of all, you must understand that your child may harbor some sense of affection for the beast. Thus, you may want to refrain from particularly gruesome tactics, such as those displayed here.

Decapitation Elmo   *Immolation Elmo*

You'll need to be somewhat more delicate and tactical to get the job done without inflicting permanent psychological damage. Luckily, there are several ways you can go about this.

For our purposes, we'll be working with the most nefarious of all the Elmo dolls: Tickle Me Elmo. If your child is very young and has yet to discover The-Voice-That-Should-Not-Be-Heard, you can simply remove the entire sound module from the beast. This will leave a perfectly cuddly and cute doll, which you may even find unrepugnant.

Beyond that, you'll need to render the creature silent in ways that won't be quite so obvious. You could just remove the batteries, but an adult accomplice could easily discover that ploy. You can buy yourself additional quiet time by installing the batteries incorrectly. For the most mechanically inclined among you, I'd suggest completely disassembling the sound module, and you'll notice a little rubber button on the circuit board that gets pressed when you squeeze his stomach. Just remove that button and enjoy the sweet, sweet silence.

Someday these draconian tactics may no longer be necessary. You may have heard that there's a company in England that offers several celebrity voices that you can use with your car's GPS system. The most popular by far is Ozzy Osbourne. If the folks at Fisher-Price want the inside scoop on the next big craze, I've got two words for you:

'ELLO, K-K-KIDS. ANY OF YOU LITTLE B-B-BUGGERS SEEN MR. (BLEEP)ING NOODLE? SHARRRONNN!!!

OzzFest Elmo

HOW TO USE THE BABY TO GET AWAY WITH JUST ABOUT ANYTHING

Difficulty ▯   *Reward* 🍺🍺🍺🍺

So much of the anticipation surrounding fatherhood focuses on the negative, like the loss of independence, the lack of sleep, and the heavy responsibility. But having a baby also presents many opportunities. We've already seen how you can score some cool stuff at the baby shower. Now let's move on and see what actually having the baby allows you to get away with.

Enjoy the Scenery

As we'll see with minivan ownership, fathers send out vibes to women that they're nonthreatening and approachable. That means that whenever you're with the baby you have a free pass to leer at all the hot chicks you want, and much of the time you'll actually get a smile in return. You may feel a brief twinge of guilt at exploiting the baby for your own lurid purposes, but he really has no idea what you're up to, and the object of your lechery gets to enjoy a little cuteness. No harm, no foul.

Be careful not to go overboard with the gawking. In particular, if the baby is hungry he may fixate on what could be the bodacious source of his next meal. If the owner of said vessels notices your baby checking out her rack, it's adorable, but if she then notices you doing the same, it's actionable.

The Look-Away

Even though having a baby makes it much easier to check out other women with impunity, every so often you will be required to take evasive action and not look directly at them. Luckily, you'll have plenty of opportunities to practice one technique that can help you out. As you learn to put the baby down to sleep, you'll soon realize that you have to avoid making direct eye contact. Otherwise, the baby gets all excited and won't fall asleep. Over time you'll learn how to turn your head away from the baby while still seeing what he's up to. Eventually you won't need this technique for the baby, but it'll always work for the babes.

Make It Funky

Sure, dealing with dirty diapers can lead to PTSD (Putrid *Tuchis* Stank Disorder), but there are certain advantages to no longer being the most malodorous member of the family. In particular, you'll no longer have to keep trying in vain to blame the dog, and you can start successfully blaming the baby. On a related topic, you can also utilize your baby's prolific gas for comedic purposes. Whenever you have guests over, sneak away under the pretext of checking on the baby. Once you're in close proximity to the baby monitor, let one fly. Now *that's* comedy!

Indulge Yourself

Yet another advantage of being an active parent is that every so often you can take a break from Pampering the baby and pamper yourself. But for whatever reason—be it genuine disinterest or a fear that they'll enjoy it a bit too much—most guys avoid beauty products and spa treatments like the English avoid orthodontics. Well, my friend, the time has come to make a change. Parenting is the perfect excuse to treat yourself to a massage or a spa treatment. Sure, you may feel dandier than a drag queen on Demerol, but what's wrong with that?

Another indulgence that most men completely overlook is skin care. Fathering is exhausting work, but Kiehl's has a line of products that can help you look and feel well rested. Stop by one of their stores (check www.kiehls.com for locations) and tell them you're a new dad. They'll walk you through everything they've got to help you out, and give you lots of free samples. The best product they have for tired dads (and moms) is their Creamy Eye Treatment with Avocado. It comes in a tiny little jar and it seems really pricey. But it lasts a long time and it's definitely worth it. You just dab a little bit under your eyes along the orbital bones, and it totally wakes up your eyes and relieves the strain from too little sleep and too much stress. Another great product is their "Ultimate Man" Body Scrub Soap, which is the closest thing to a loofah that I can recommend to any but the most heterosexually secure men.

On a related note, having a baby is also an excellent excuse to update your wardrobe. I strongly recommend that you forego the classic white or blue dress shirt in favor of earth tones, which will more closely match the inevitable baby food stains. I believe Perry Ellis has something in a breast milk beige, and there's a very nice Calvin Klein shirt in sweet potato ochre. As far as ties go, your best bet is to go with something borderline psychedelic, such as anything from the Jerry Garcia line. There's no way anyone would ever spot the spit-up on those designs.

Teenage Self   *Fatherhood Self*

Or Just Let Yourself Go

Not to worry, my friends, none of the aforementioned refinements are mandatory. In fact, if you want to take the exact opposite approach to personal hygiene, the baby allows for that as well. Don't feel like shaving for a few days? Fine, just blame your scruff on the baby. No time to pick up your dirty clothes from the floor? That's the kid's fault, too. Feel free to push this strategy as far as you can—you may ultimately regress to the slovenly state of your teenage self—just keep in mind that the more disheveled you become, the more actual fathering you'll be expected to do.

Boy's Toys

You can, and should, use the baby to justify any and all high-tech and electronics purchases. There's obviously a need for a new camera and maybe a photo printer for the computer, but there's also so much more:

NETFLIX

The one certain casualty of parenthood is the movie night. My wife and I didn't see a single movie in a theater during our son's first year. When we did finally start getting a regular babysitter, we wanted to hang out together rather than sit silently in a movie theater. Netflix (www.netflix.com) is great for making sure you've constantly got new DVDs around whenever you get a moment's peace. Plus, they make it easy to keep track of all the movies you want to see, which becomes difficult as parenthood renders you more and more brain-dead.

DVR

This is probably the greatest invention since self-adhesive stamps. You can easily program it to record everything you want to watch, including every episode of a show throughout the season, and fast-forward through every commercial when you watch what's recorded. Most importantly, the DVR lets you pause live TV, so when the baby starts screaming at the absolute worst time, you won't miss a thing.

NOISE-CANCELING HEADPHONES

Sure, you could just get earplugs when the kid starts a-wailing, but this is such a cool product you should definitely check it out. The risk here is that you'll start to use them at less appropriate times, like just after sex or whenever your in-laws are in town. The best product on the market is probably the Bose QuietComfort headset, which detects the ambient noise and emits a corrective signal to negate the noise so you hear almost nothing. Yes, they're expensive, but when did that ever stop you from buying something you don't really need? Now if only they would invent stink-canceling noseplugs.

A GIANT TV

Now we're getting into uncharted territory, so only the bravest among you should consider pressing on. Although the American Academy of Pediatrics does not recommend any television for children under the age of two, I recently discovered a loophole that you may be able to exploit for your own personal satisfaction. Just as many SUVs are so big that they're not regulated as passenger cars, thus allowing automakers to avoid certain quality and safety regulations, so may an oversized TV be so big that the child doesn't even recognize that it is a TV. You can plop your baby down at the base of your new 61-inch PlasmaSync PX, and he'll get some vague impression that there's something going on above his head, but he won't realize that it's worth watching. As an added bonus, the TV will come in a humongous box, which will make a great playhouse.

WEBCAMS

This is such cool technology, and you can be up and running right away for just a few bucks. Webcams allow you to do live video chats with friends and family using your existing Internet connection. The quality of the video isn't great (it'll remind you at times of the moon landing), but it's getting better and better all the time. Right now, the best overall program to use is MSN

Messenger. I've found that the other instant-messaging software programs just don't work as well, and the programs you have to pay for aren't yet worth the cost.

Stick It to the Man

At some point we've all been frustrated by women who use their feminine charms to avoid a speeding ticket or some other citation. Well, my friend, you need fret no more. With a handy-dandy infant in the backseat, you, too, can be free and clear of any unsightly infractions. As the police officer approaches your car, set that baby off a-cryin' by any means necessary (short of physical discomfort, that is). Take away his favorite toy, or offer him a snack and then withhold it. Once the baby is crying hysterically, put on your best frazzled-daddy expression (and a tear or two couldn't hurt). Apologize profusely to the officer and tell him or her that you've had a cranky kid in the car all day and need to get him home and to bed. Odds are he'll let you off with a warning and a kindly pat on the head.

A Built-In Excuse

Don't forget that having a baby gives you an easy out for any and all miserably boring social and family events that you would otherwise have to attend. Plus, if you find yourself at an event and you need an escape strategy, you can always use the baby to cut out with impunity. For example:

- We'd love to come to Phoenix in August for the wedding, but the baby has a chronic ear condition and can't fly until after Labor Day.
- Sure, bring out the next box of vacation photos. [*Take*

baby's favorite toy away.] Oops, the baby's just about to melt down. We should really get going.

• Normally you wouldn't be able to keep us away from tonight's all-accordion recital, but the baby's got projectile diarrhea and we're busy hosing down the nursery.

You see, it's just that easy.

The Right of Way

Finally, you'll want to take full advantage of the deference people pay to a parent and child. You can pretty much use the stroller to brush aside any pedestrians and pets that would dare to cross your path. We talked about how flying with a baby, while difficult and taxing, also presents certain advantages. You can also use the baby to cut ahead in line at the store, grab a seat on the subway, and use the car pool lane on the freeway.

HOW TO FEEL MANLY IN A MINIVAN

Difficulty   *Reward*

"Hey, Chili, is this your ride?"
"Yeah, I like to sit up high, check everything out. I mean, it is the Cadillac of minivans."

—MARTIN WEIR (DANNY DEVITO) AND CHILI PALMER (JOHN TRAVOLTA), *GET SHORTY*

So your better half has suggested that instead of buying the latest Enormo-Cruiser SUV with the optional cow-catcher, retina-searing high beams, and twin-tap kegerator, you should consider a minivan for you and your fledgling posse. She'll tell you that minivans get better mileage, produce less pollution, and are safer for their occupants and other drivers alike, plus lots of other emasculating gibberish. And even though your wife is obviously more mature, intelligent, considerate, and probably better-looking than you deserve, you'll still find it difficult to concede to buying one of those uninspiring "eunuch-cycles."

Let's face it, none of those arguments matter, because the real reason you want the SUV is because you think it makes you look cool. I mean, the guys in all those commercials, they're rugged outdoor types who grab life by the horns and take no prisoners. They're real men. You, of course, do not live in a car commercial. You're married with children, and no ridiculously excessive amount of horsepower will change that. And yet you can't let go of that adolescent desire to look cool, right? I'm not saying you should. So in your never-ending quest to find a car that makes you look cool, it's time you asked yourself one important question: Look cool to whom?

If you're trying to impress your buddies, an SUV is overkill. Remember, these are the guys who still think you're wicked cool for belching the entire *Three's Company* theme back in college. Worried they'll give you shit for driving a minivan? Aren't these the same guys who still give you shit because three summers ago you failed to fit an entire grapefruit in your mouth? Face it, as far as your buddies are concerned, an SUV won't tip the balance in your favor, and a minivan is just one addition to the endless list of things for which you'll receive crap from your comrades.

It's not about the guys, though, is it? It's about the chicks. Since the invention of the automobile, men have been using their cars as an accessory to attract women. But you're married and wouldn't think of cheating on your wife. For most married men, of course, it's not cheating that's important; it's thinking that you could actually find a living, breathing human woman with whom to cheat if you so choose. So you think the SUV will make the chicks think you're something other than just some domesticated shlub who works in a cubicle and wears brown socks and sandals while mowing the lawn every Saturday? Here's a newsflash for you: Most women in the real world (as opposed to those you'd see on *The Real World*) are more attracted to the guys in the minivans than to the guys in the SUVs.

Think about it. A minivan is like a wedding ring. It shows that you're a responsible, mature guy who's not caught up in the whole chest-pounding macho thing. Remember Christie Brinkley in the red Ferrari going after Chevy Chase in the Family Truckster in *National Lampoon's Vacation*? You see, it's true.

Of course, that doesn't mean you have to settle for a minivan that you think is totally lame. Conceding to buy a minivan means that you've earned indisputable license to trick it out with every cool option your giddy sales guy can throw at you, and your wife can't really object. Always wanted a 6-CD changer? They can tuck one in right behind the navigation system. Can't imagine a road trip without multizone temperature control, DVD monitors, and an in-dash frozen daiquiri machine? You got it. And if the model you're looking at offers a smart key (so you can unlock the car without taking your keys out), definitely get it, since it's something that's both really cool and is truly essential when you're trying to get into the car with a baby in one arm and a bag of groceries in the other.

Still not feeling manly? Here's one last thing to try: Why not pimp out that mutha minivan with Gear Vendors overdrive, chrome-plated demon race carbs, Edelbrock manifold, Detroit lockers, and Cragar mags, a Panhard rod rear suspension, and, of course, a Billet aluminum cigarette lighter. And don't forget, lifters never go out of style. BOO ya!

HOW TO NOT BLATHER ON AND ON ABOUT YOUR KID

 Difficulty    *Reward*

(for everyone around you)

"Jack, you're a grown man. You're in control
of your own words."
"You're goddamn right I do. Now here come two
words for you: Shut the f%^& up!"

—JONATHAN MARDUKAS (CHARLES GRODIN) AND
JACK WALSH (ROBERT DENIRO), *MIDNIGHT RUN*

I'm including this chapter for purely selfish reasons, since I find incessant parental blather about as pleasant as nails on a chalkboard or anything uttered by Tara Reid. Before I had a kid, I couldn't hide my contempt every time some parent would go on and on about how great their kid was, and how he was going to be a soccer star, and how he was just a genius, and so on. When I'd get caught rolling my eyes, they'd say something like, "Just wait until you have kids, you'll do the same thing." Well, I've got news for you, I don't do the same thing, and you don't have to, either. You have control of your own words, and you never need to conform to some baby-boutique ideal of how a parent is supposed to act, talk, and spend (see "How to Maintain the Illusion of Control"). There is a fine line between being a proud parent and being a blithering idiot, so let's take a moment to learn where that line is, and how to avoid stepping over it.

Parents talk about their kids constantly, often to the exclusion of all other topics, and there's nothing inherently wrong with that. I realized shortly after becoming a father that not all of that talk is the same. There are basically three types of parent talk: the completely understandable, the delightfully heartwarming, and the incredibly annoying.

The Completely Understandable

I was unaware of the "completely understandable" form of parent talk until I became a parent myself, and then I heard it everywhere. It consists of the commonplace chat about what the baby is doing, whether he's eating and sleeping, and how the parents are coping with any ailments or oddities about the child. It may sound to the untrained ear like normal conversation, but it's really a cry for help. It doesn't quite sound like bragging, but you do assume that someone would have to be terribly self-centered to think that anyone would be interested in the mundane minutiae of their everyday lives. It turns out they're not talking just to hear themselves talk; there actually is a purpose. Basically, all parents at some point talk about their babies and themselves just so they can get some reassurance from other parents that they're not totally screwing up. You might mention how often the baby poops and then check the faces of everyone within earshot to make sure they show some expression of consent. It may seem totally neurotic, but all new parents are totally neurotic for at least a month. And that's why this type of talk is fine by me.

The Delightfully Heartwarming

This is the best type of parent talk. It stems from a genuine amazement at how this little creature is progressing before their very eyes. Parents will say things like, "It's just miraculous that one day he wasn't able to crawl, and then the next day he just put it together." They're not bragging about their particular child, they're expressing their awe at the development process in general. And the fact is, it is a truly amazing thing to watch. The only problem is that the "delightfully heartwarming" can morph into the "incredibly annoying" all too easily.

The Incredibly Annoying

Very simply, this type of parent talk stems from the parental delusion that their child is somehow uniquely gifted and is somehow developing in a more impressive way than every other child. The fact is that virtually all babies go through the same exact process. Some do it a little slower than others, and some skip certain steps or show a particular acumen for certain skills. In the end, though, no single baby can corner the market for miraculous development.

A subset of the "incredibly annoying" is the "ridiculously extrapolated." Everyone has witnessed this, with reactions ranging from polite nodding to derisive snorting. Little Jimmy loves staring at the computer, so he's bound to be the next Bill Gates. Little Suzie loves her heart-shaped pillow, so she's destined for cardiology. Sure, parents dream about their children's destinies all the time. Just keep it to yourself, or I'll be forced to remind you that your kid's ubiquitous plumber's crack suggests an alternate future career.

Ultimately, the only way to avoid becoming incredibly annoy-

Hold That Thought

The most common form of incredibly annoying parental blathering deals with the child's alleged genius. These parents don't just embody the Lake Wobegon embellishment that "all the children are above average." If their delusions of brilliance were correct, all the children would be little Einsteins. I suppose you can't blame parents for believing that their kids are brilliant, but some fascinating new research suggests that they shouldn't count their eggheads, because there's a catch.

A recent study from the National Institutes of Health suggests that the smartest children develop their intelligence later than other children. Brain scans show that the cortexes of the very smartest children start off thinner than those of other children, but eventually develop more quickly and for a longer time, until by around age eleven the smartest kids have thicker cortexes. The theory is that later development allows more complex stimuli to shape the brain, and ultimately make the child into a smarter adult, whereas children who start out smarter than average may peak in high school and end up like Al Bundy.

Basically, what this means is that having a "genius" baby isn't necessarily something to brag about.

ing is to just not be so. Focus on how amazing it is that all babies go through this same complex development, and how privileged you are to be able to witness it firsthand. If you start thinking your kid is somehow more amazing than all the other kids (as you no doubt will from time to time), just try to keep it to yourself. And if you just can't resist, and you start to blather on insufferably about your kids, allow me to quote Bobby De Niro: Shut the f%^& up!

Epilogue

HOW TO CELEBRATE THE KID'S FIRST BIRTHDAY RIGHT

Difficulty   *Reward*

Well, you made it. The baby's almost a year old. You survived conception, pregnancy, delivery, night feedings, mutant baby illnesses, teething, separation anxiety, hundreds and hundreds of diaper changes; projectile vomiting, projectile peeing, and a few other projectiles that still keep you awake at night; rolling and crawling and maybe even walking; depression and exhaustion, frustration and panic. All that, and I'll bet you wouldn't trade it for anything.

Was I right? Is your life back to "normal," and can you hardly imagine what life was like before the baby? It's amazing how it all works. You throw yourself into an epic undertaking, with no idea what you're doing and no clue how it will all turn out. And yet, hour after hour and day after day, you've adjusted, figured things out, and done what you had to do. After all is said and done, the baby's asleep and you're sitting in bed finishing up this silly little book. It just wasn't all that difficult, right? Be careful how you answer that, since the person sitting next to you might just get the idea in her head that she's ready to go through it all over again. Here's a great way to distract her:

Lean over and give her a big smooch. Tell her you're canceling the baby's birthday party and instead you're going to get the grandparents to babysit for the weekend and the two of you are going anywhere she wants to go. After all, nobody deserves a first-birthday present more than you guys. Have a great time, forget about the kid for a few days, and sleep in as late as you possibly can. Just be careful, or you may find out why so many siblings are born about a year and 9 months apart. And you know what they say: once you have that second kid, everything changes.

And just so you're prepared when the kid finds out you stiffed him on his first birthday, stuff what little remaining cash you have left into the therapy jar.

If you think having a baby is scary, try going to Barnes & Noble and figuring out which baby books you should buy. It's totally overwhelming. To help you out, here are just a few books that I found to be particularly helpful along the way. I'm not saying that you absolutely must read all of them, or even any of them. But take a look and see if any will work for you. At the very least, make sure your wife knows about them. She'll probably find them more essential than you will, and you'll score points for being involved in the whole process.

TAKING CHARGE OF YOUR FERTILITY
by Toni Weschler

My wife and I didn't anticipate any problems getting pregnant, but we read this book anyway. Not only does it include fascinating information regarding the biology of conception, it provides a simple method for using that information to increase your chances of getting pregnant. And, most importantly, it provides a sense of control during a process that can seem intimidating, random, and beyond your control.

THE GIRLFRIENDS' GUIDE TO PREGNANCY
by Vicki Iovine

This is just an great all-around book for wives to read during pregnancy. It's informative, insightful, and funny. Most important, it doesn't focus on everything that could possibly go wrong, like *What to Expect When You're Expecting*.

THE HAPPIEST BABY ON THE BLOCK: THE NEW WAY TO CALM CRYING AND HELP YOUR NEWBORN BABY SLEEP LONGER by Harvey Karp

This magical little book provides a simple, effective technique for soothing a fussy newborn. You should definitely have these tricks in your arsenal shortly after the baby arrives, as I can pretty much guarantee they'll come in handy. If only they would keep working until the kid is a teenager.

THE BABY OWNER'S MANUAL: OPERATING INSTRUCTIONS, TROUBLE-SHOOTING TIPS, AND ADVICE ON FIRST-YEAR MAINTENANCE by Louis and Joe Borgenicht

This is an excellent little book, packed with tons of information, from the people who brought you the *Worst-Case Scenario* books. Not only is it full of great information about how to take care of your baby, it presents the information clearly and precisely, with just enough humor to keep guys interested.

FULL CATASTROPHE LIVING: USING THE WISDOM OF YOUR BODY AND MIND TO FACE STRESS, PAIN, AND ILLNESS by Jon Kabat-Zinn

If you've never meditated before, having a baby may be just the stressor you need in your life to convince you to start. This is a brilliant, accessible introduction to the practice. Kabat-Zinn keeps everything grounded in reality, and offers simple instructions to get you started.

GOOD NIGHT, SLEEP TIGHT: THE SLEEP LADY'S GENTLE GUIDE TO HELPING YOUR CHILD GO TO SLEEP, STAY ASLEEP, AND WAKE UP HAPPY by Kim West and Joanne Kenen

I think this is the best and most important book you'll read about parenting. Whether your baby sleeps well or not is probably the single greatest determinant of your level of enjoyment with the whole process. This book is remarkably well-researched, offers very structured methods for working with your baby at different ages, and never talks down to you or assumes you have a perfect child. I can't tell you how many times my wife and I were facing a particular sleep issue, and this book not only anticipated it but offered consistently effective solutions.

ACKNOWLEDGMENTS

Thanks so much to everyone who helped out along the way: Laurie Abkemeier for her ceaseless enthusiasm and guidance; Ben Sevier, Marc Resnick, John Karle, Jen Crawford, Joe Goldschein, and everyone at St. Martin's; Jay Mazhar for his wonderful illustrations; Gracia Walker and the good folks at Kiehl's; Sandesha Tendulkar, who developed the new daddy workout and saved my aching shoulder; all the midwives at the UCLA Birthing Center; Caroline and Ben's folks; Colin's ma and pa; Jill "Hot Mama" Connor; Nick's mommy and daddy; Mohan's mother and father; Uncle Chris; Luke and Harrison's parents;

ACKNOWLEDGMENTS

Izzy and Becka's ma and pa; Mikayla and Caden's folks; Noah's mother and father; Zach's parents; Lucie and Violet's mom and dad; Dylan's mommy and daddy; Sophie and Alexandra's folks; Asher's ma and pa; Samantha's mother and father; Jason "Big Papi" Soslow; Danielle and Jaime's parents; Jimmy and Glen's mama; and the gals at the Dog House.

Thanks and love to Grandma Margaret and Grandpa Martin, Sammy Atticus-Mayday Hunter's folks, and my own dear old dad. And, of course, to Corinne and Azi, who make everything feel so right.

Azi's daddy is a supercool guy, with devilish good looks and a rapier wit. He is the author of *How to Iron Your Own Damn Shirt: The Perfect Husband Handbook* and *The Hemingway Cookbook*. He and Azi's mom live with the boy in Santa Monica, California.